Ultima
REALISTIC ROCK

by CARMINE APPICE

MW00851844

This new edition is dedicated to my mother, Mary N. Appice

Original oil painting of cover design: Arlene Lawin

Distributed by
Alfred Music Publishing Co., Inc.
P.O. Box 10003
Van Nuys, CA 91410-0003
alfred.com

Printed in USA.

ISBN-10: 0-89724-486-9 (Book & CD)
ISBN-13: 978-0-89724-486-2 (Book & CD)

Contents

	Page	CD 1

Contents   Page   CD 1

A click track is included to help guide you along as if you
were actually playing in the studio! Feel free to choose any
of the exercises from the book you like and have fun
applying these patterns to the songs!

Note: Tracks 13 and 14 are from the CD
     DBA Derringer, Bogert, Appice titled **Doin' Business As**
     Track 15 is taken from **Carmine Appice's Guitar Zeus II** CD

CD 2

CD CREDITS

CD produced by Carmine Appice for Bianic Music
Recorded at Sound Asylum
Digital editing and engineering by Steve (The Lunatic) Werbelow

FOREWORD

Welcome to the ULTIMATE REALISTIC ROCK DRUM METHOD! I have added many new exercises and applications to this edition that will make it the most complete rock book ever!

There are now two CDs for you to listen to the grooves and exercises and play along with.

Odd time signatures will no longer be a challenge. The 7/8 and 9/8 sections will have you playing them as easily as 4/4.

The combinations (hand and foot) section will explore more double bass (double pedal) patterns using your China cymbals in a variety of musical situations.

The play-along songs have been recorded without drums so that you can now practice and apply your favorite *Realistic Rock* patterns.

I have added more albums on my discography and updated my endorsements for you to see.

All of this, along with all of the classic exercises from the original *Realistic Rock* book and the updates, creates an exciting new dimension for you to learn how to play rock drums!

Now you can become one of the many great drummers who have gone through *Realistic Rock*—drummers like Dave Weckl, Greg Bissonnette, and Vinny Appice, just to name a few.

I hope this book continues to help drummers of all ages around the world just like the original book has done in the past. Now let's ROCK!

Carmine Appice

_____ **Part 1**

Key To The Book

This book should be practiced at a slow tempo, at first. Then, as it becomes easier, bring the tempo up, little by little. Every exercise in the book is in 4/4, so the 4/4 time signature at the start of each exercise has been eliminated.

At the beginning of each exercise each line is marked for easy identification.

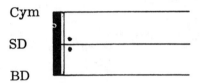

Cym

SD

BD

- Legend:
     Cym = Ride Cymbal or Hi-Hat Cymbals
             (Either can be used . . . it is up to you, unless specified.)
     SD = Snare Drum
     BD = Bass Drum

At the end of each exercise is a repeat sign 𝄇 which means repeat once. Some exercises will be played at least eight times. The more you play the exercise, the better you'll get!

Now let's go to the note values which are used in this book!

Note Type:			Length of Beats:
Quarter Notes . . . . ♩	=		1 Beat
Eighth Note. . . . . ♪	=		½ Beat
Sixteenth Notes . . . . ♬	=		¼ Beat
Thirty-second Notes . . . . . ♬	=		⅛ Beat

- How to Count:
     ♩ = 1   2   3   4
     ♪ = 1 & 2 & 3 & 4 &
     ♬ = 1 e & a 2 e & a 3 e & a 4 e & a
     ♬ = No counting system; just "feel it" against the sixteenth note count.

Eighth notes are twice as fast as quarters.
Sixteenth notes are twice as fast as eighths.
Thirty-second notes are twice as fast as sixteenths—that is how to feel thirty-seconds instead of counting them. All rest values are the same and will be explained as they are used.

Part II deals with eighth notes on the cymbal, quarter and eighth notes between hand and foot. Part II is the elementary part of the book.

At the end of Part III is a 12 bar exercise. To get the feel of playing different rhythms side by side, this exercise was designed as a collage of all the rhythms played up to that point. It's a review in the form of a drum solo. You'll find such exercises at the end of each part.

If possible, all exercises should be played at the drum set to get the right rhythmic feel and the correct balance needed for tonal separation.

18 Ways To Use This Book

Here are eighteen ways to play the rhythms in this book. First play each exercise as written. Then play one of the ways shown below by matching the hand rhythms (numbers 1 - 6) with the Hi-Hat rhythms (letters A - C). Any rhythm pattern that has eighth notes on the right hand (left hand for left-handed drummers) can be varied this way.

HAND RHYTHMS
1. As written (right hand on
          cymbal)
* 2. Backwards (left hand on
          cymbal)
3. Right hand on quarter notes
* 4. Backwards on quarter notes
          (left hand on cymbal))
5. Right hand on the "&"
6. Backwards on the "&"
          (left hand on cymbal)

HI-HAT RHYTHMS
A. Hi-Hat on quarter notes

B. Hi-Hat on eighth notes

C. Hi-Hat on "&"

* "Backwards": right handed drummers play left hand on the ride cymbal; left handed drummers play right hand on the ride cymbal.

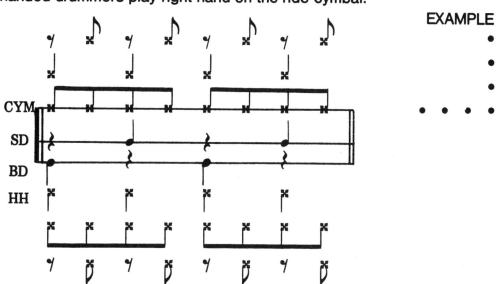

EXAMPLE

4/19/17

Some exercises, such as polyrhythms, cannot be varied because the ride cymbal or Hi-Hat hand is playing set patterns. For polyrhythms, play the A, B and C patterns on the Hi-Hat (worked by foot).

Part 2

CD 1

TRK 1

Quarter Notes

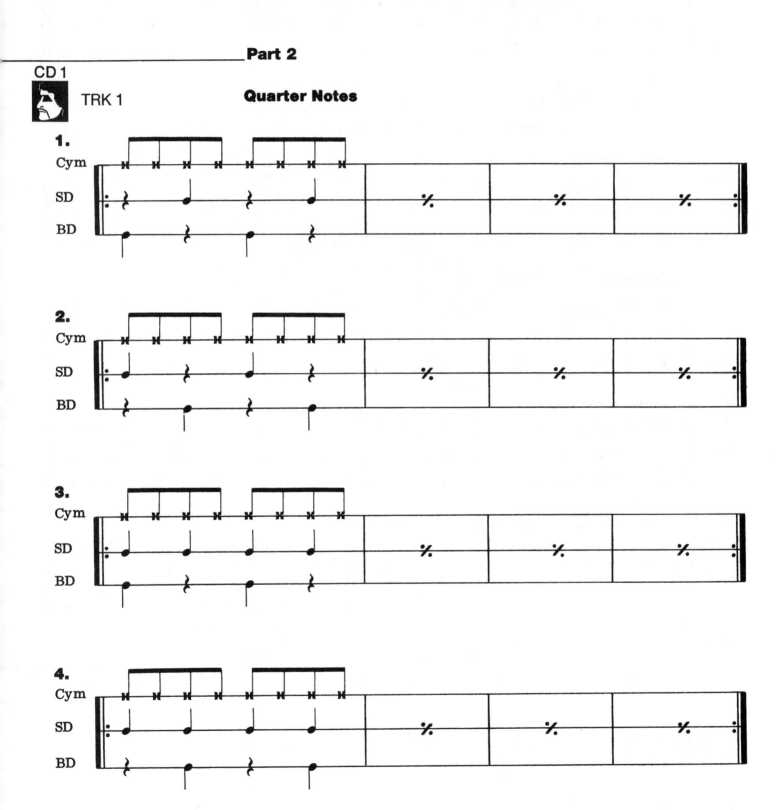

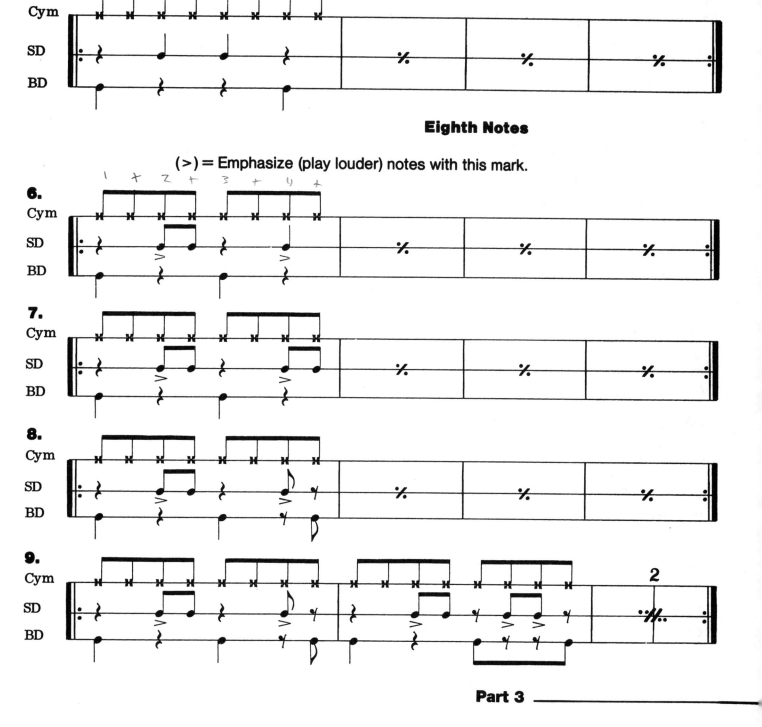

Eighth Notes

(>) = Emphasize (play louder) notes with this mark.

Part 3 ———————————————————

Accented Bass Drum

In this exercise, accent the bass drum by playing on the "&" of the beat. This kind of accent is called an "off" kick.

• • • • • • • • • • •

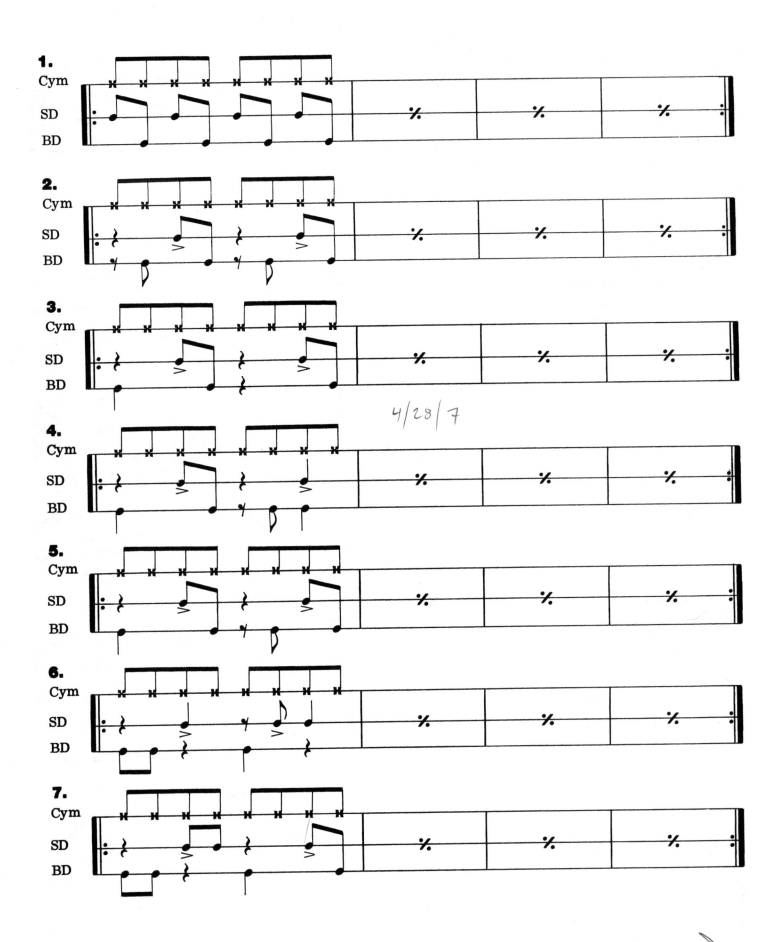

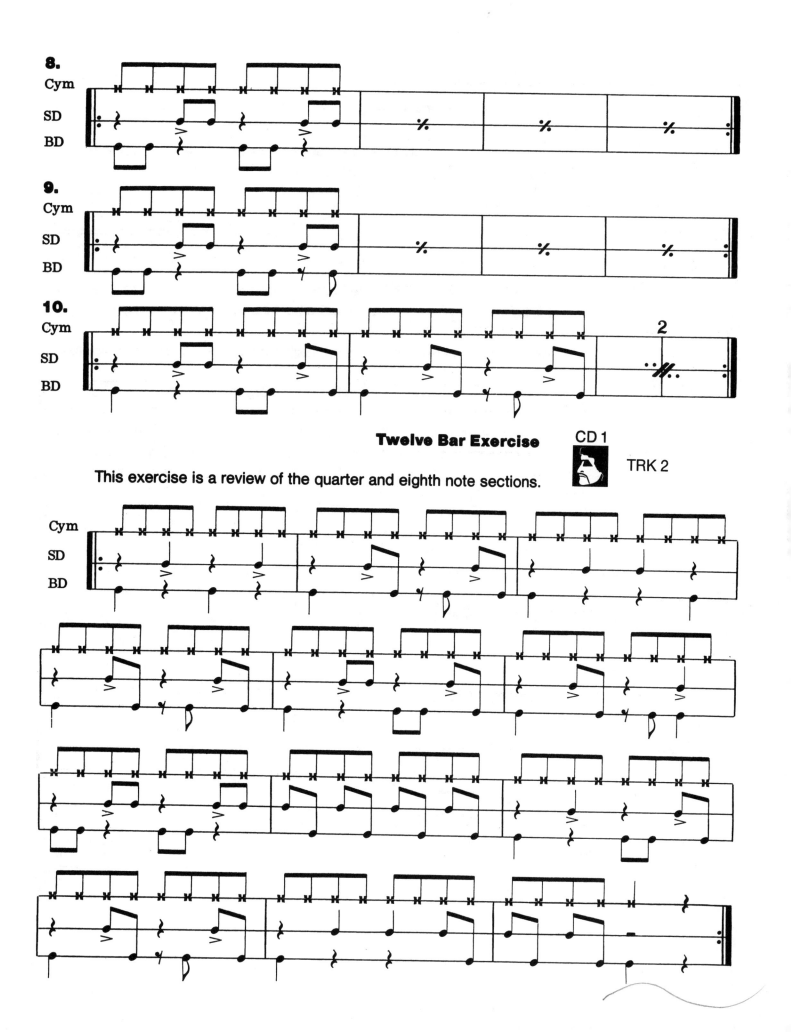

Twelve Bar Exercise

CD 1

TRK 2

This exercise is a review of the quarter and eighth note sections.

Part 4

Sixteenth Note Rhythms

Rock drummers rely heavily on sixteenth notes. The count for a set of 16th notes is  Each set of four 16th's is equal to one quarter note:

A 16th note rest has the same value as a 16th note—¼ of a beat. In this figure , count 1-e-&-a but hit only the last three notes. A rest can be anywhere in the figure. Eighth note rests can also appear.

This section also introduces the dotted eighth and sixteenth: . The dot increases the value of the preceeding note by one half. Since an eighth note equals two sixteenth notes, a dotten eighth equals three sixteenth notes. A dotted eighth and a sixteenth add up to one beat. Count the figures like this: or . This rhythm is played with a bounce.

Another figure used in this section is

This is a syncopated rhythm.
Hit on 1, e. Rest on &. Hit on a.

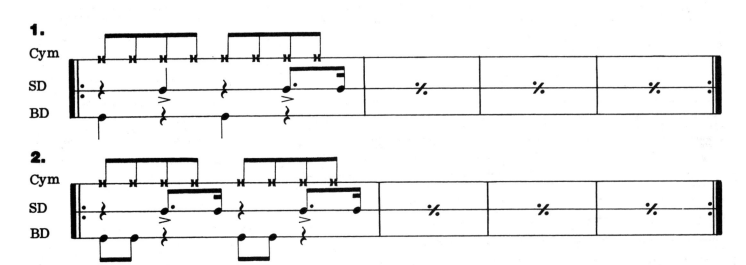

Eight Bar Exercises In Sixteenth Notes

More Sixteenths

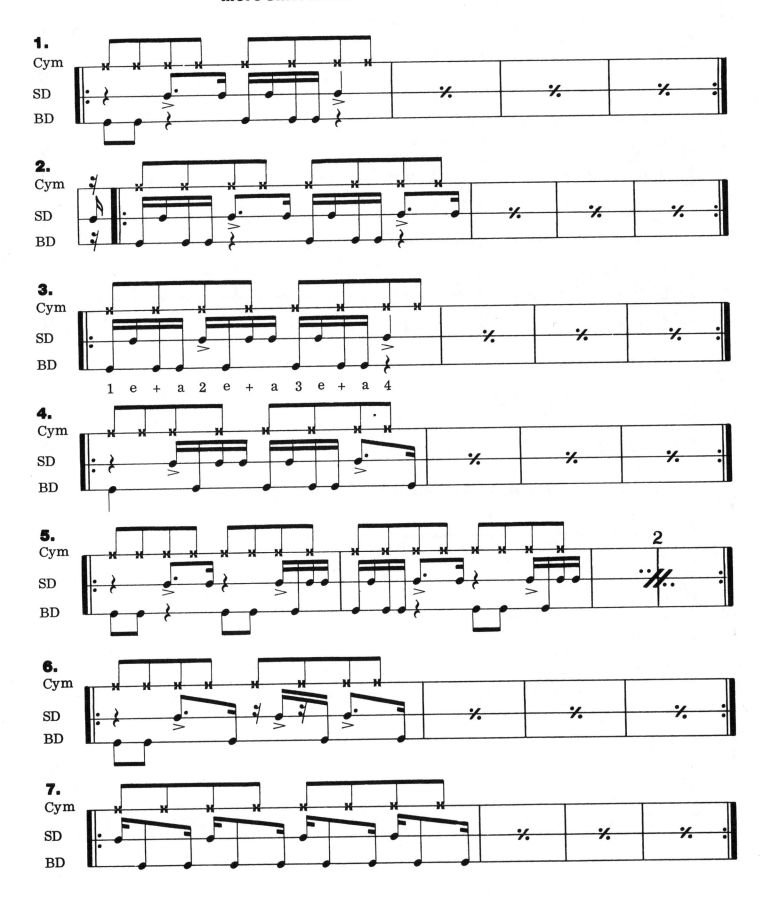

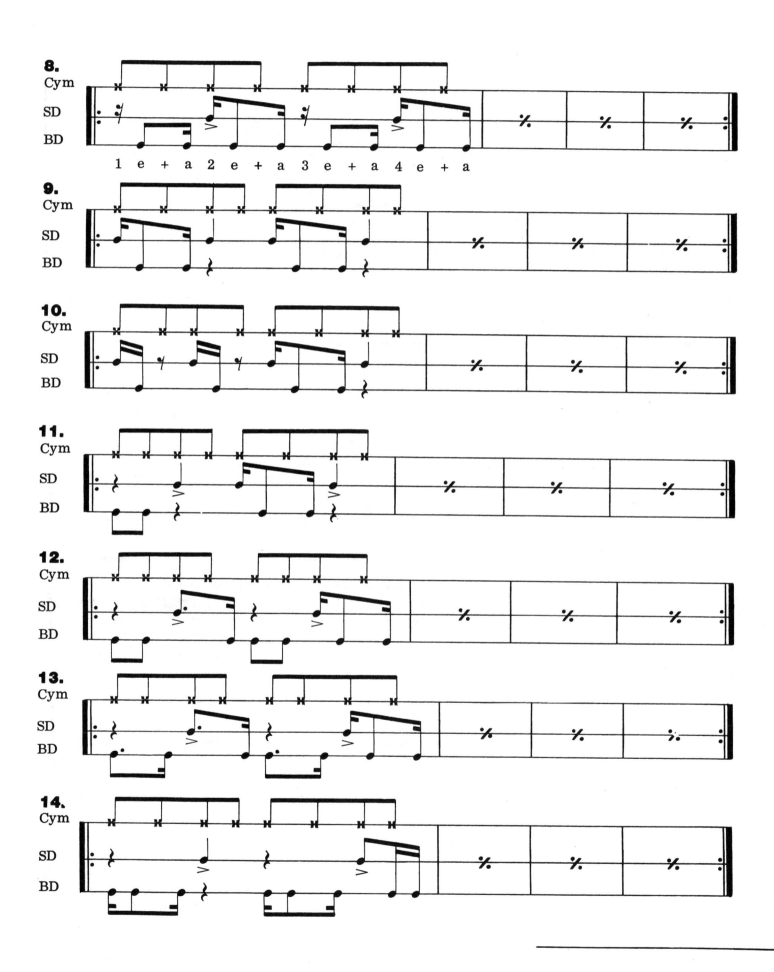

15.

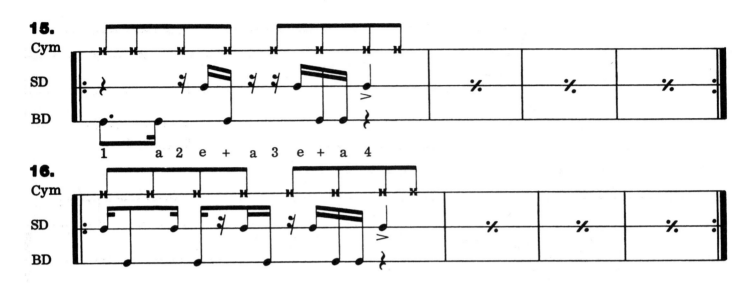

16.

Twelve Bar Exercise — Sixteenth Notes

This exercise should be played slowly at first.

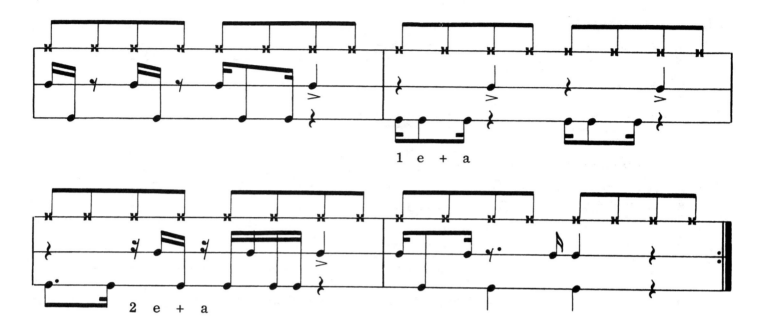

Part 5_____

CD 1

TRK 4 **Sixteenth Note Triplets**

 Two groups

Sixteenth note triplets are counted: 1 ti ta + ti ta   of sixteenth

note triplets equal two eighth notes: The secret for reading sixteenth
note triplets is simple. The first 16th note of the triplet is usually left out:

therefore, the triplet fits between the eighth notes that are being played on
the Cymbal. Example:

          Sixteenth note triplet figures are
easy to play if this is kept in mind. The only possible problem—a fast, basic
beat—can be solved by playing these exercises very slowly. Gradually
increase the tempo.

1.

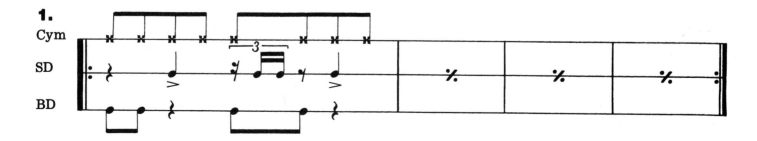

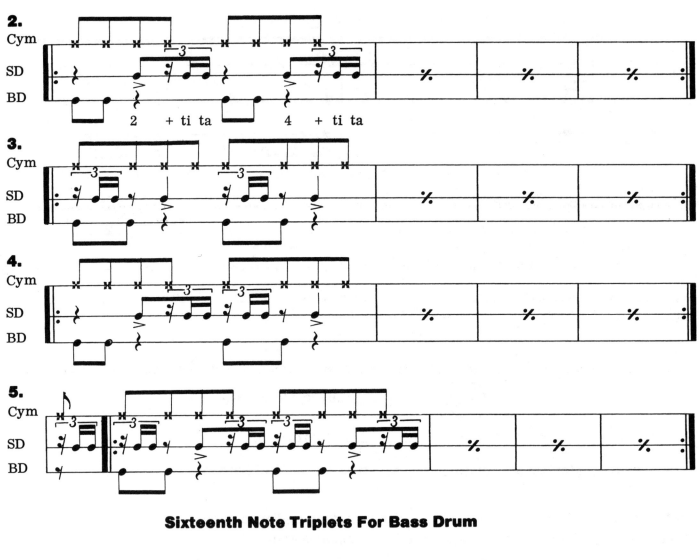

Sixteenth Note Triplets For Bass Drum

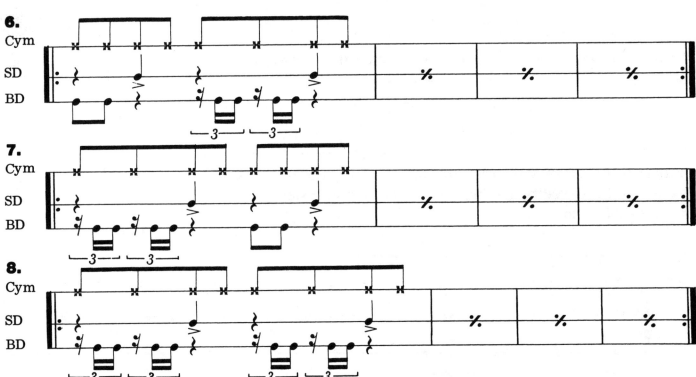

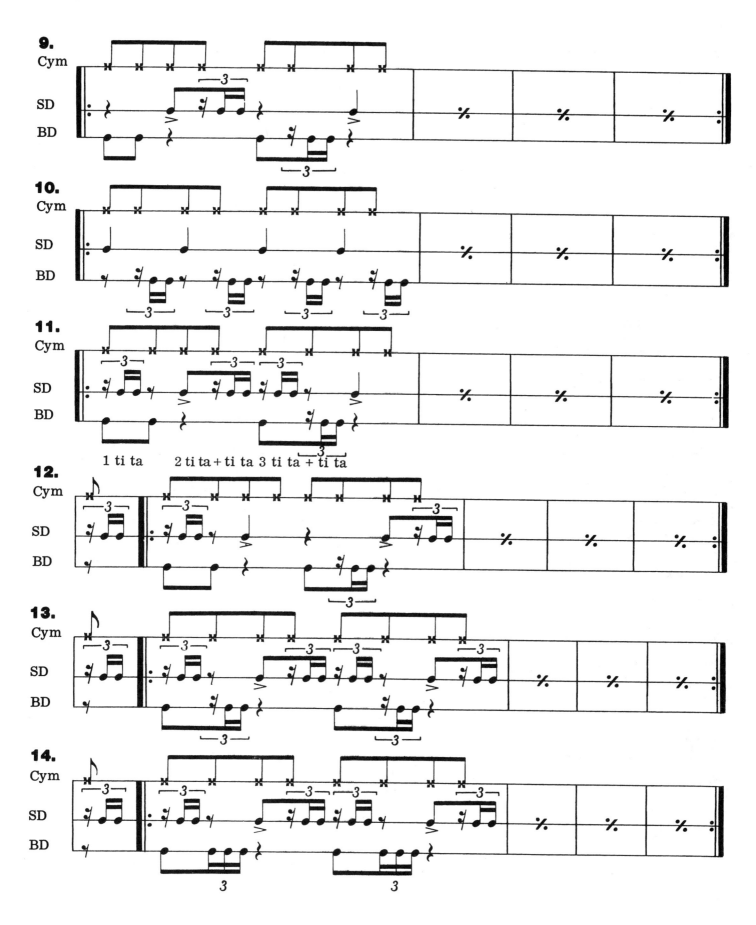

9.

10.

11.

1 ti ta   2 ti ta + ti ta 3 ti ta + ti ta

12.

13.

14.

15.

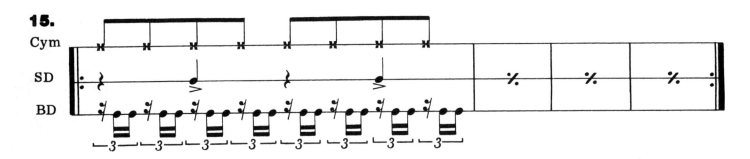

Twelve Bar Exercise

Sixteenth Note Triplet

The next pages will be a combination of all the rhythms learned up to this point, plus some new ones. You should be able to play these if you learned the preceding exercises.

CD 1

Part 6  TRK 5

Review Exercises

The following exercises will develop one's ability to improvise on the rhythms previously learned. In this section the rhythms appear in 12, 14 and 16 bar exercises and solos. Play these slowly at first. Repeat at gradually faster tempos.

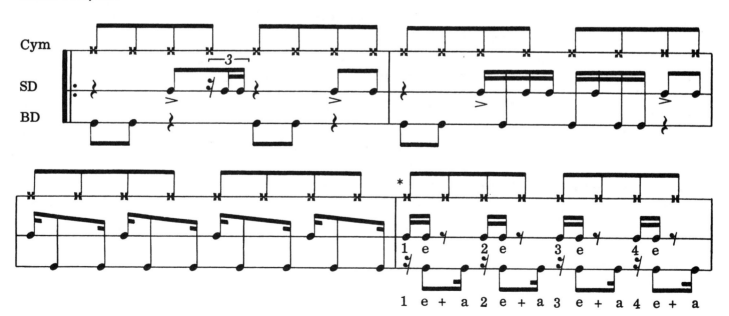

1 e + a 2 e + a

*Keep same foot rhythm as preceding measure and double snare drum figure—count is 1 e 2 e 3 e 4 e for snare drum.

Sixteen Bar Exercise

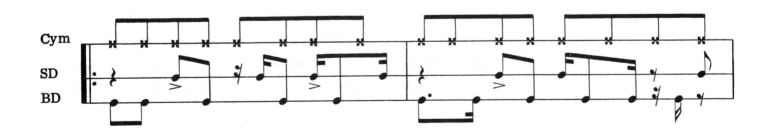

Changing Bass Drum Patterns

Sixteen Bar Solo Using Hand On 2 And 4

Steady Four On The Snare

Part 7

Syncopation

CD 1

TRK 6

Syncopation is an off-beat rhythm. Beats that are not usually accented are now emphasized; the rhythm is broken up. The hard presence of the 2 & 4 after-beat disappears, but is still felt. Syncopation is used in musical styles as divergent as rhythm and blues and hard rock.

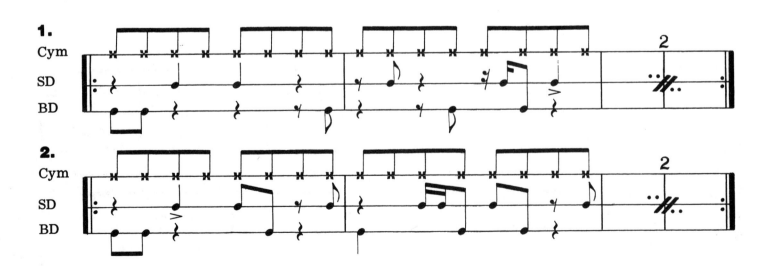

3.

4.

5.

*Half note rest ( ) gets two full beat rests.

6.

7.

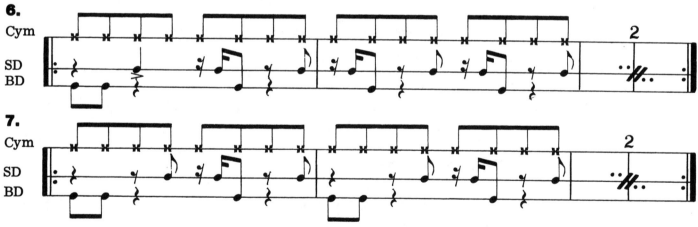

Sixteen Bar Exercise

This 16 bar exercise could easily be used as a drum break in a song with this type of feel.

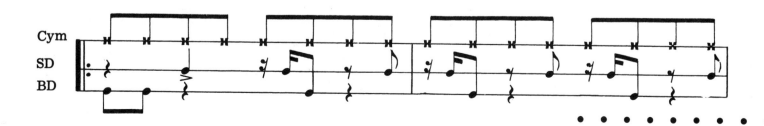

. . . .

Two Bar Breaks

Syncopation is usually played in 2 to 4 measure sequences, followed by the original rhythm.

1.

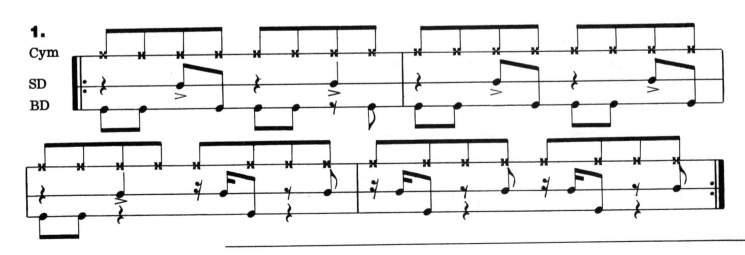

Part 8 _____

Hi Hat Rhythms

In recent years many original variations have been added to the standard repertoire of Hi-Hat rock rhythms. The Hi-Hat studies in parts VIII and IX will cover both the old and the new.

+ = closed
o = open

Study the vertical and horizontal relationship of the notes on all lines. Notice that as the Hi-Hat opens and closes, a more complete, rhythmic sound is created

Remember to play these slowly at first. Repeat at gradually faster tempos.

CD 1

Basic Eighth Note Hi-Hat Rhythms TRK 7

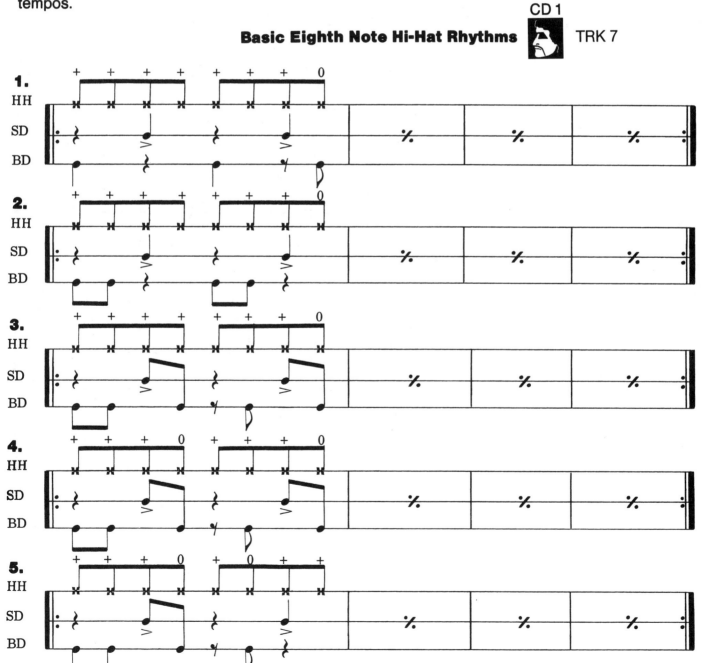

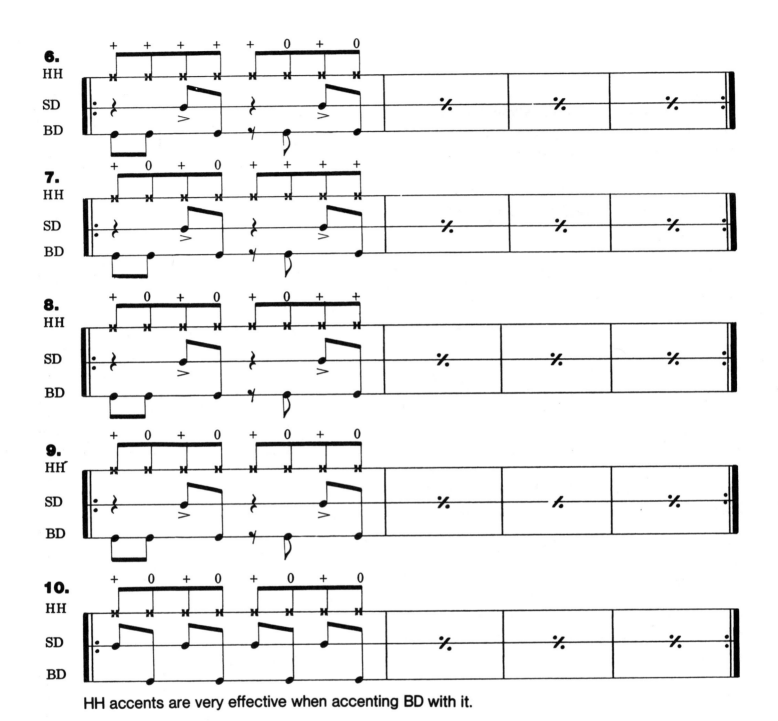

HH accents are very effective when accenting BD with it.

Slightly Syncopated

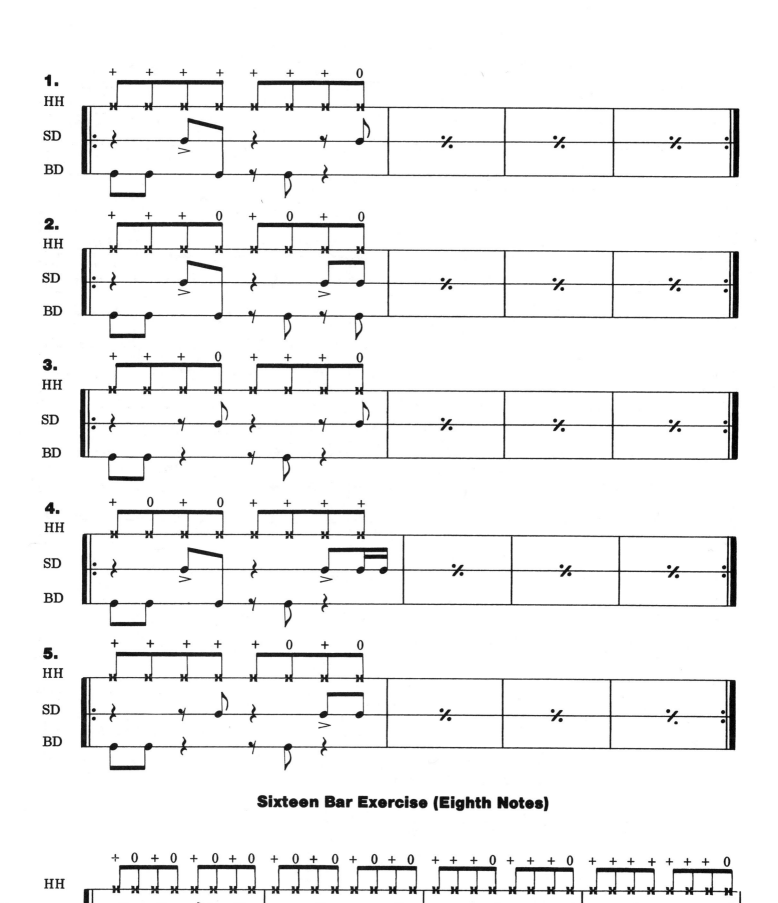

Sixteen Bar Exercise (Eighth Notes)

Sixteenth Note Hi-Hat Rhythms

Play HH sixteenths on closed Hi-Hat Cymbals.

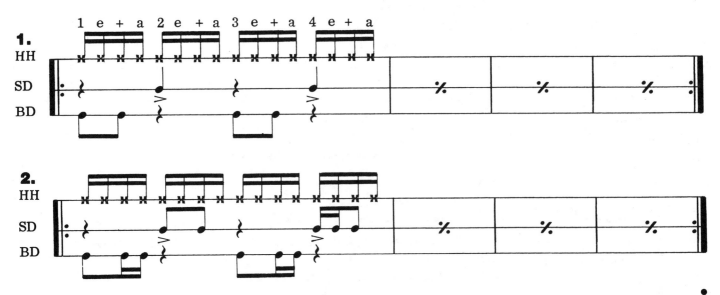

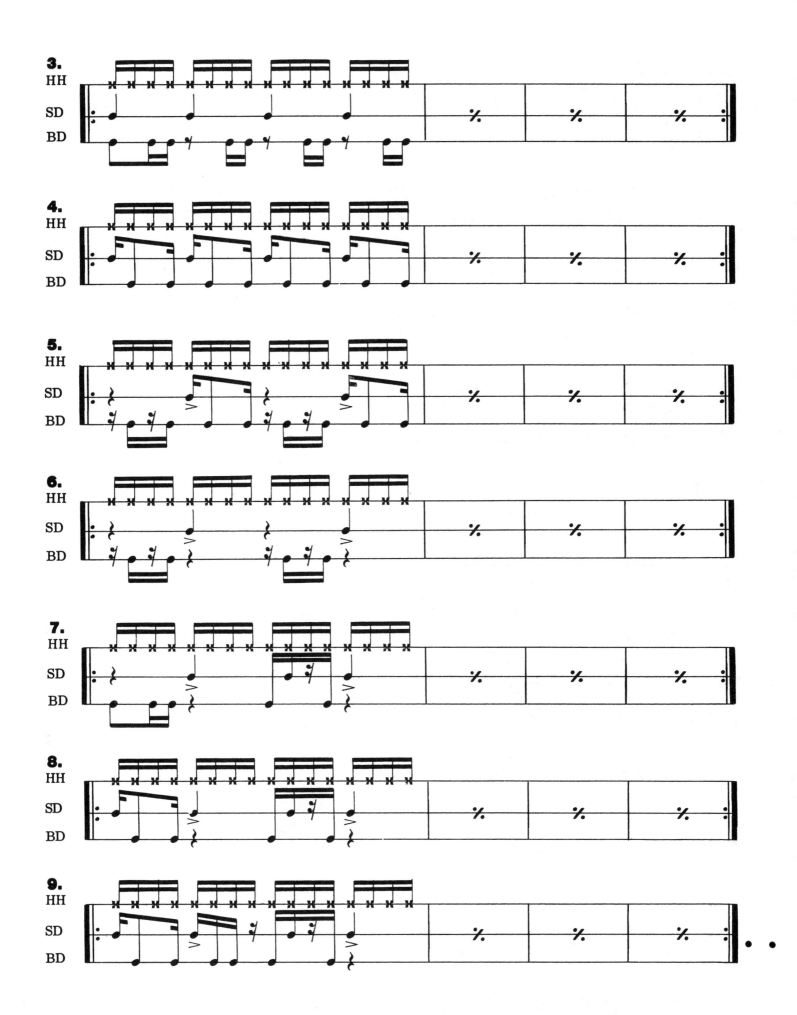

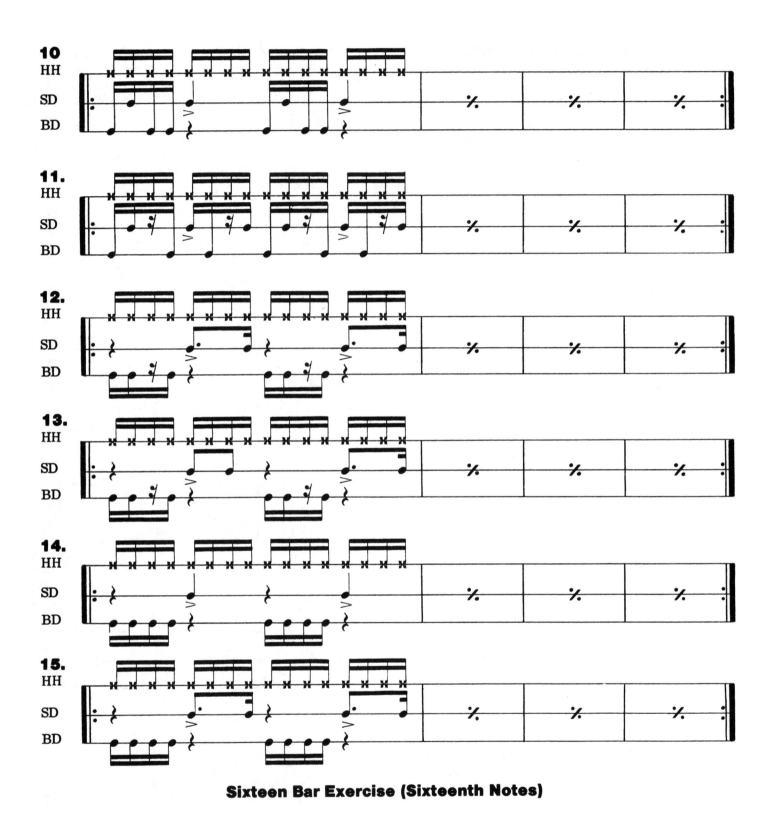

Sixteen Bar Exercise (Sixteenth Notes)

Play HH sixteenths on closed Hi-Hat Cymbals.

Sixteenth Notes — Accented — Open And Closed

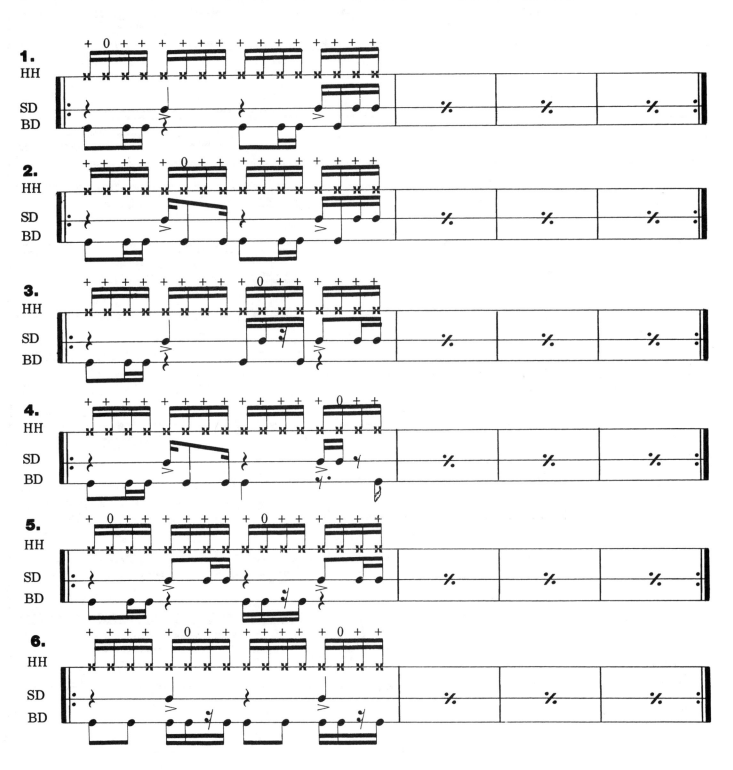

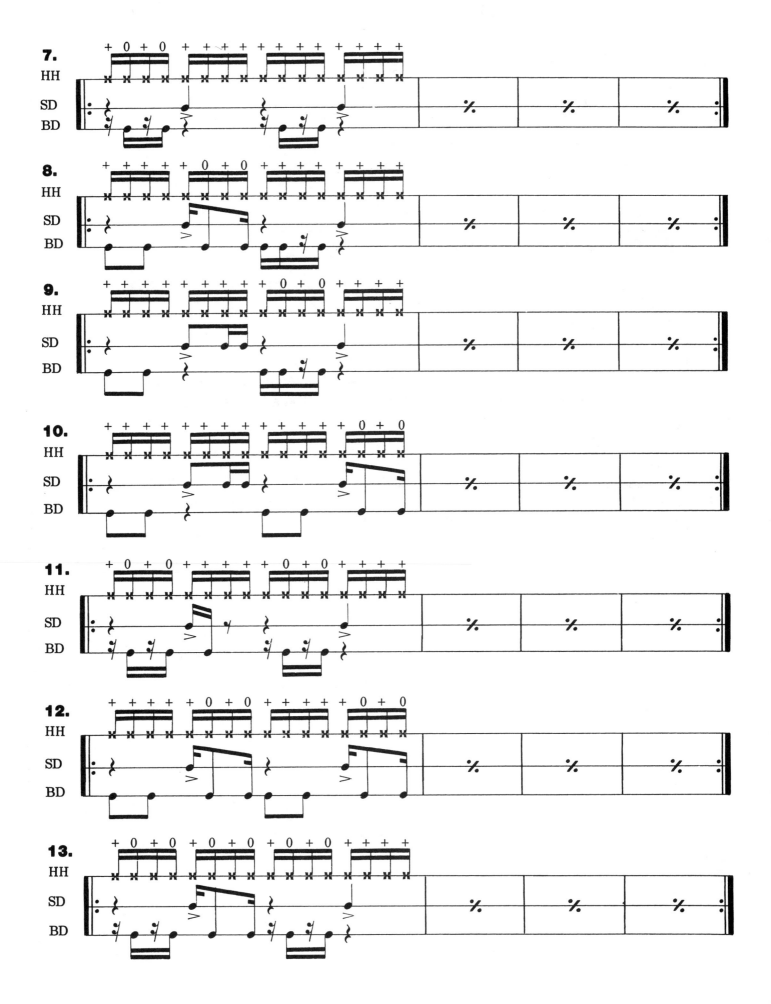

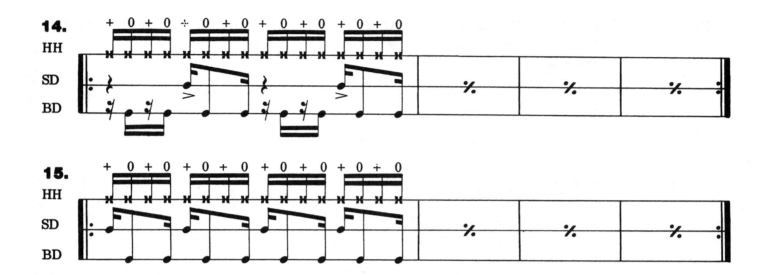

12 Bar Exercise

The following is a twelve bar exercise of accented sixteenth notes with the Hi-Hat opening and closing. The accent occurs when the cymbals are played in the open position.

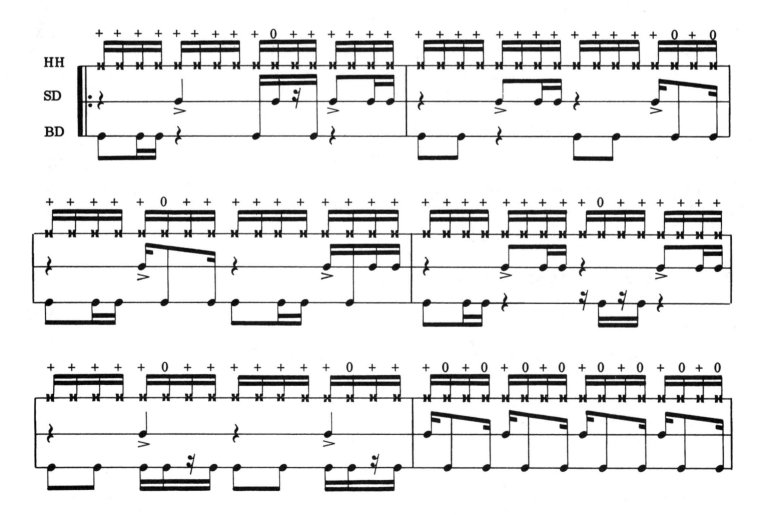

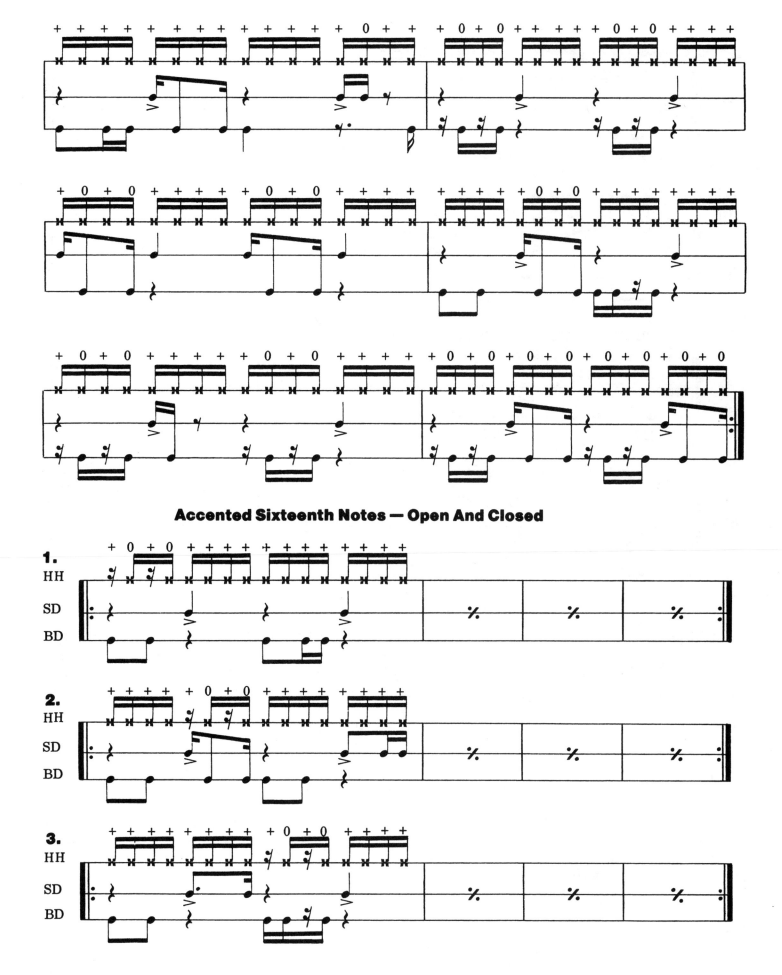

Accented Sixteenth Notes — Open And Closed

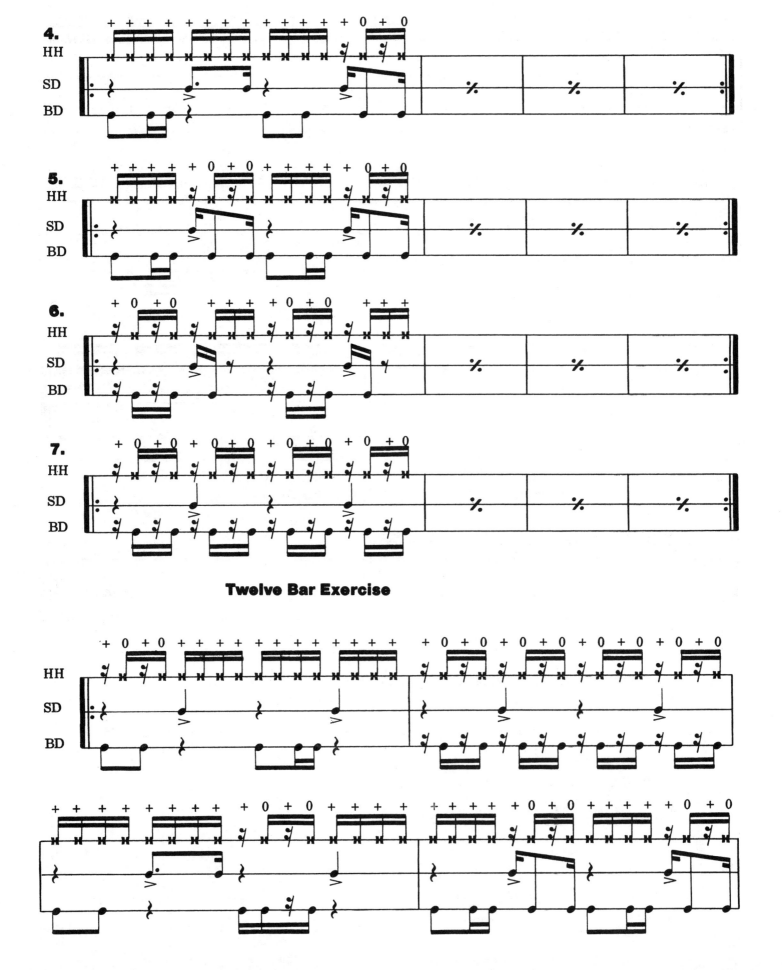

Twelve Bar Exercise

Advanced Sixteenth Note Rhythms

Exercises 1-5 are played on the HH and SD using alternate stickings.

CD 1

TRK 8

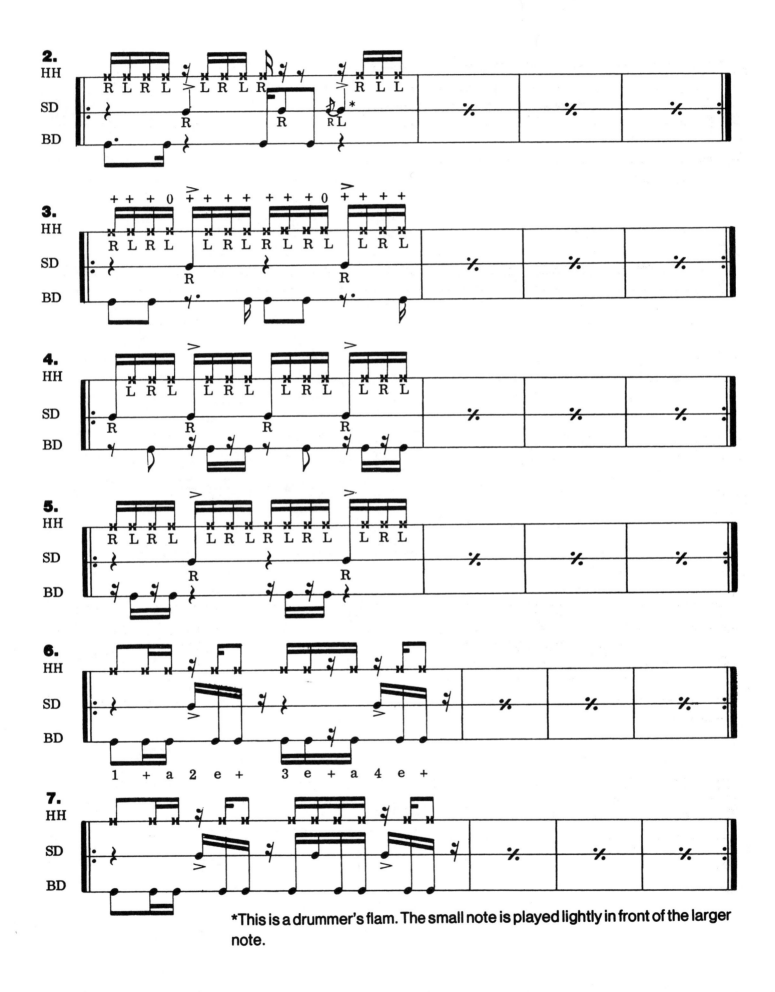

*This is a drummer's flam. The small note is played lightly in front of the larger note.

8.

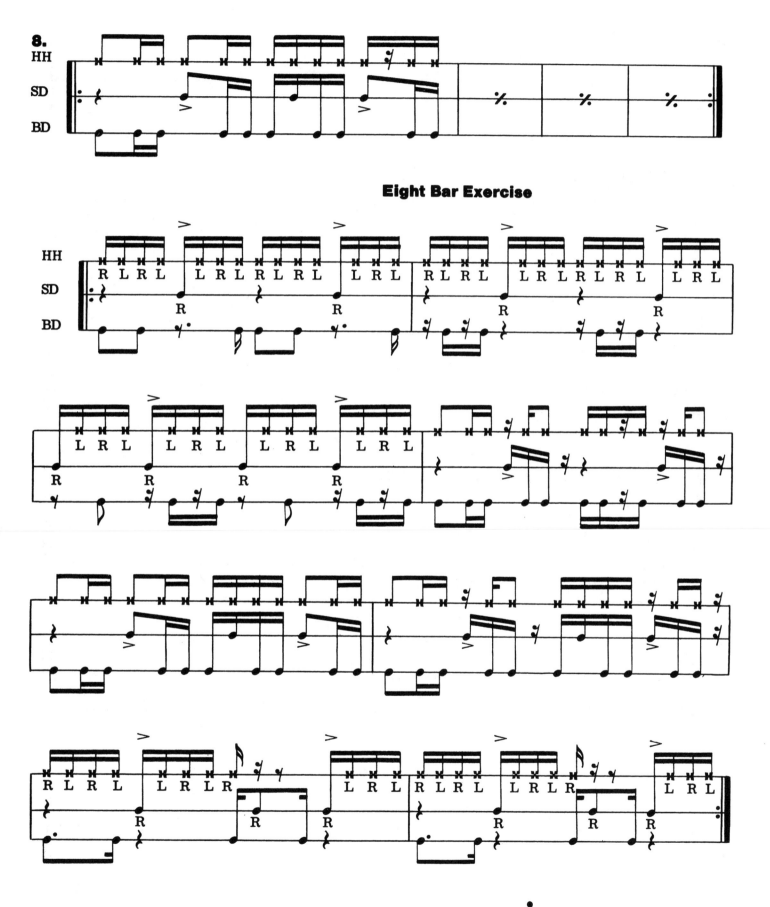

Eight Bar Exercise

CD 1

TRK 9 **Rock Poly-Rhythms**

In these exercises the right foot plays the same pattern as the right hand!

Right hand on cymbal or Hi-Hat ( )
Left hand on snare drum   ( )
(Left-handed drummers should reverse the sticking.)

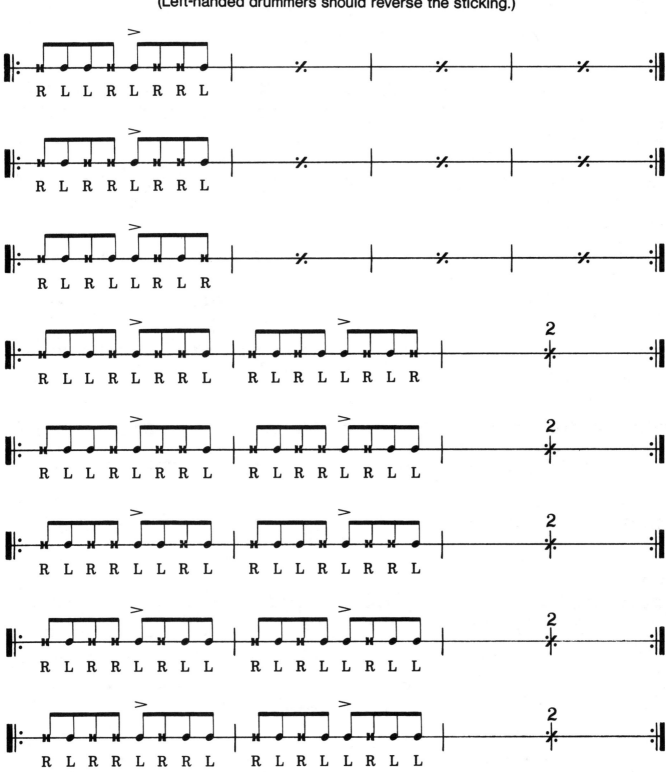

Part 9

Review

All the rhythms in parts II-VIII are covered in this review.

These exercises can be played as professional rock solos in 14 or 16 bar breaks. The cymbal line can be played on either the ride cymbal (RC) or Hi-Hat cymbals (HH) except where specifically noted for HH (+/o).

Sixteen Bar Solo 2.

Sixteen Bar Solo 3.

Sixteen Bar Solo 4.

Part 10

CD 1

TRK 10

Shuffle Rhythms (Bounce)

To create a bounce feeling, the shuffle rhythm uses dotted eighth and sixteenth notes between hands and feet. Quarter notes are played on the cymbal, instead of the usual eighths. The natural emphasis is on 2 and 4.

Dotted Eighths And Sixteenths

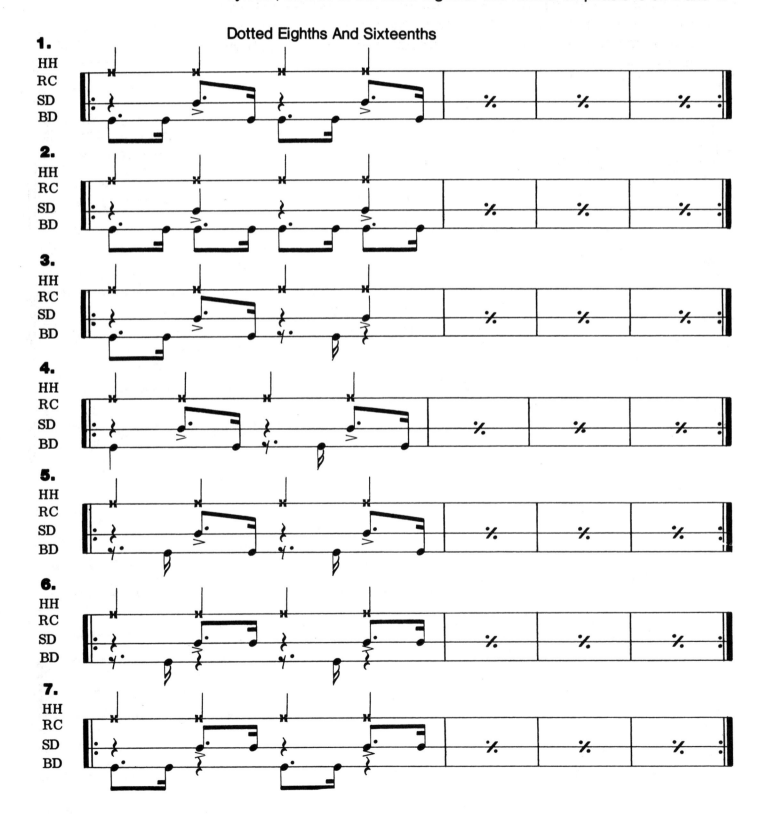

8.

Triplet Ruffs

The sixteenth note triplets on this page are part of an embellishment known to drummers as a "ruff." In the following exercises, triplets are played against quarter notes on the cymbal. In this section, eighth note triplets are counted:

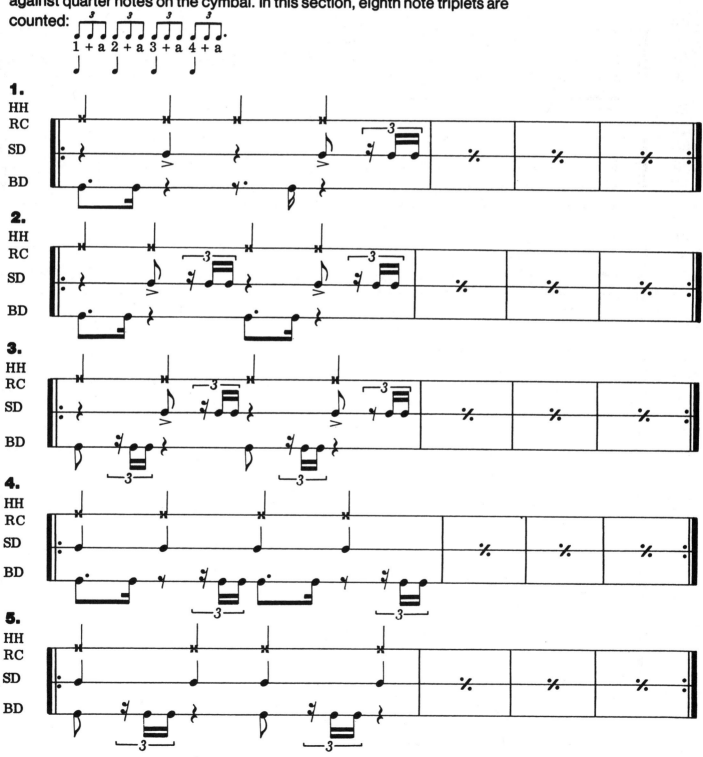

Eighth Note Triplets For Bass Drum

8.

Sixteen Bar Exercise

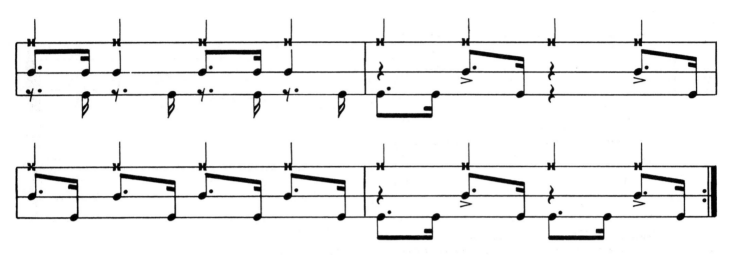

Shuffle Rhythms

These shuffle rhythms are played with dotted eighth and sixteeenth notes, rather than quarter notes, on cymbal. Improvising occurs between the snare and bass drum.

Dotted Eighth and Sixteenth On Top

Improvising on Snare and Bass Drum

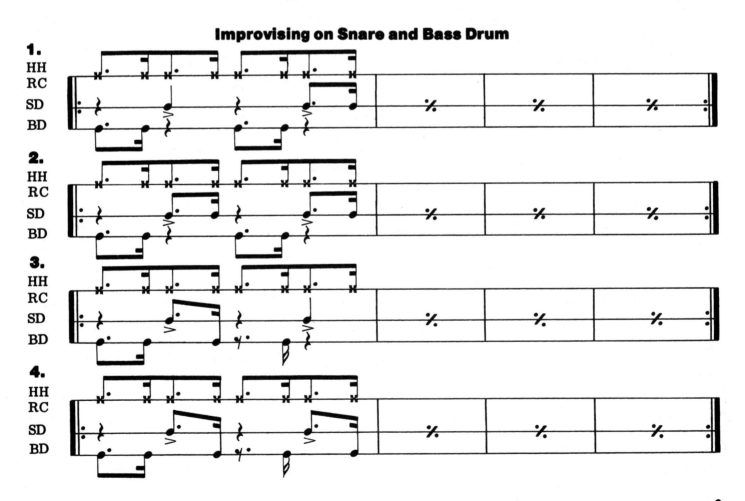

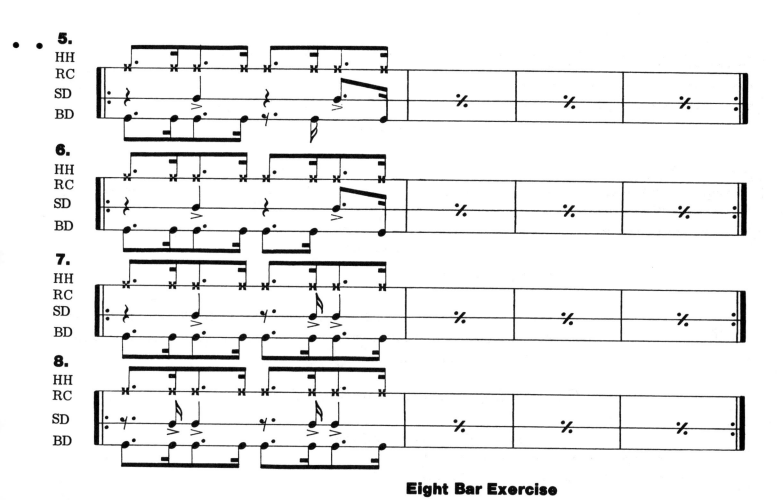

Eight Bar Exercise

Dotted Eighth And Sixteenth Notes

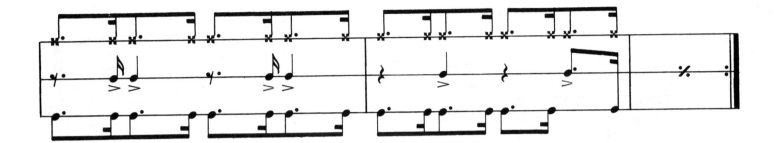

Part 11

Rock Fills

Here are a number of fills that I use. They can be easily adapted for any playing situation. The drums are marked at the beginning of each line as follows:

RC	Ride Cymbal
ST	Small Tom-Tom
SD	Snare Drum
LT	Large Tom-Tom
BD	Bass Drum

Sticking choice is dependent upon physical set-up and musical inflection.

Stickings which have worked well for me are indicated with R and L.

One Bar Breaks

The first measure is the fill. The second measure shows the standard rhythm that might come before and after the fill.

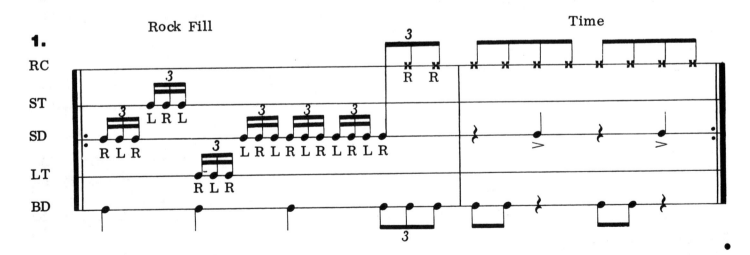

6.

7.

Two Bar Breaks

The first two measures are the fill.

Rock Fill

Time

1.

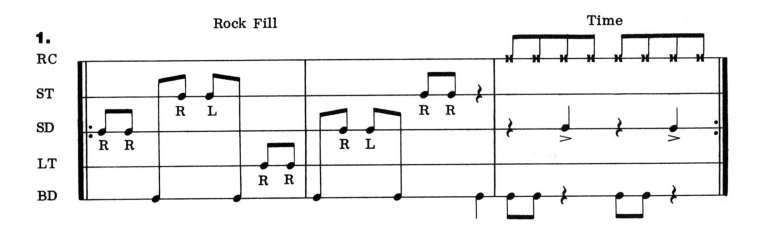

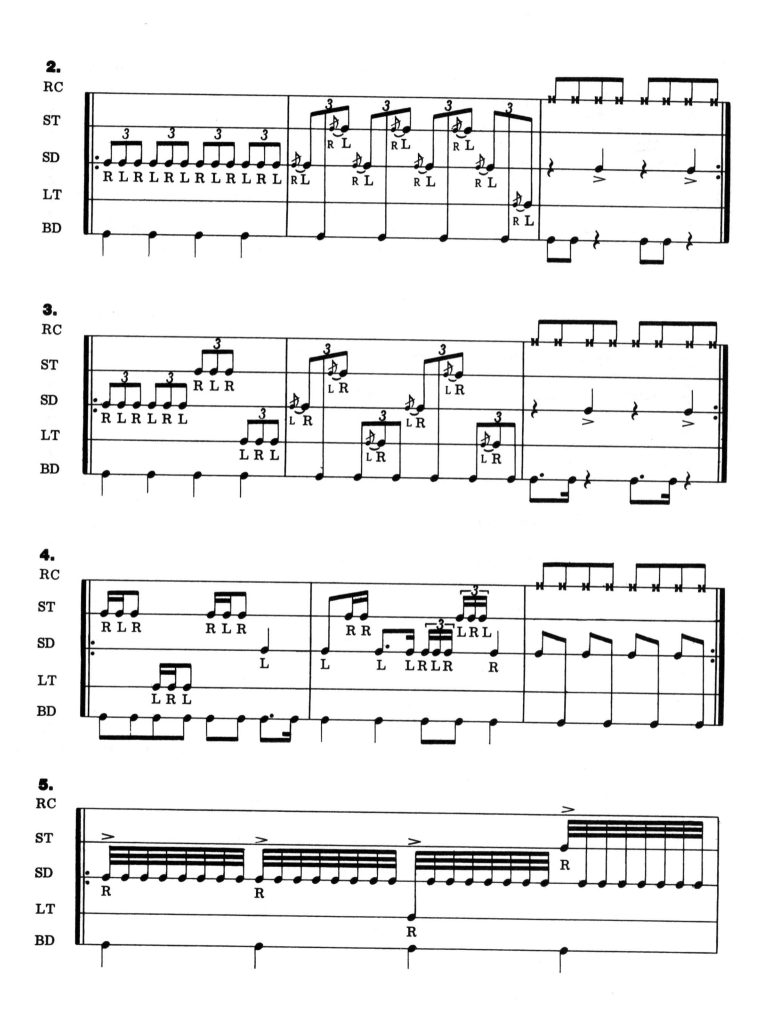

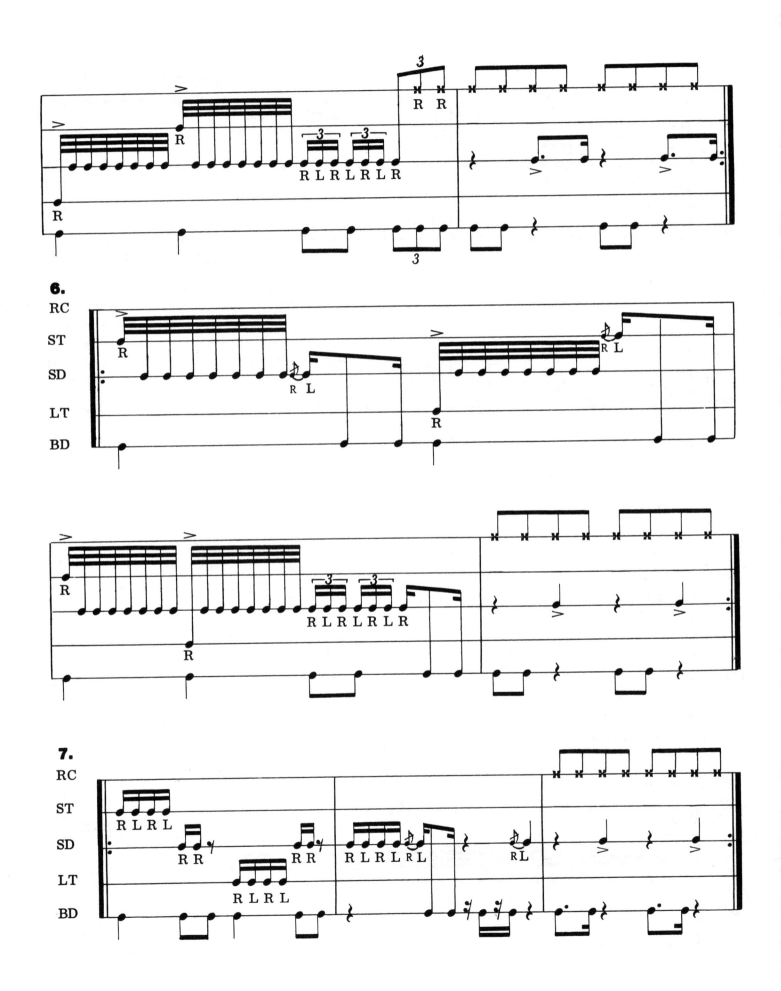

8.

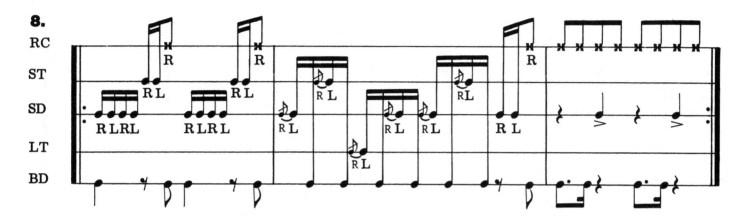

Part 12

Double Bass

CD 1

TRK 11

Double bass drumming is not as hard as it looks—it's just like adding another line to the music.

Example•

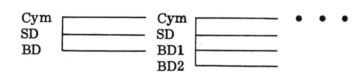

Use the ride cymbal as indicated. BD1 is the main bass drum (right for right handed drummers, left for left handed drummers) and BD2 is the second bass drum. Look at relationships. Figure out the rhythms. Take it slow!

Using Quarter Notes on BD2

1.

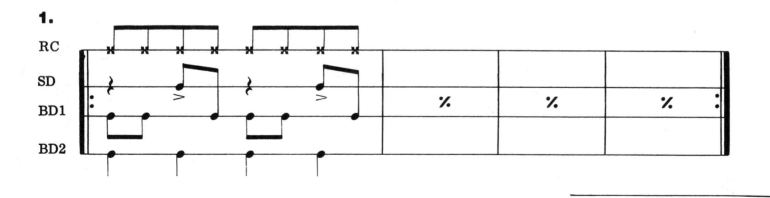

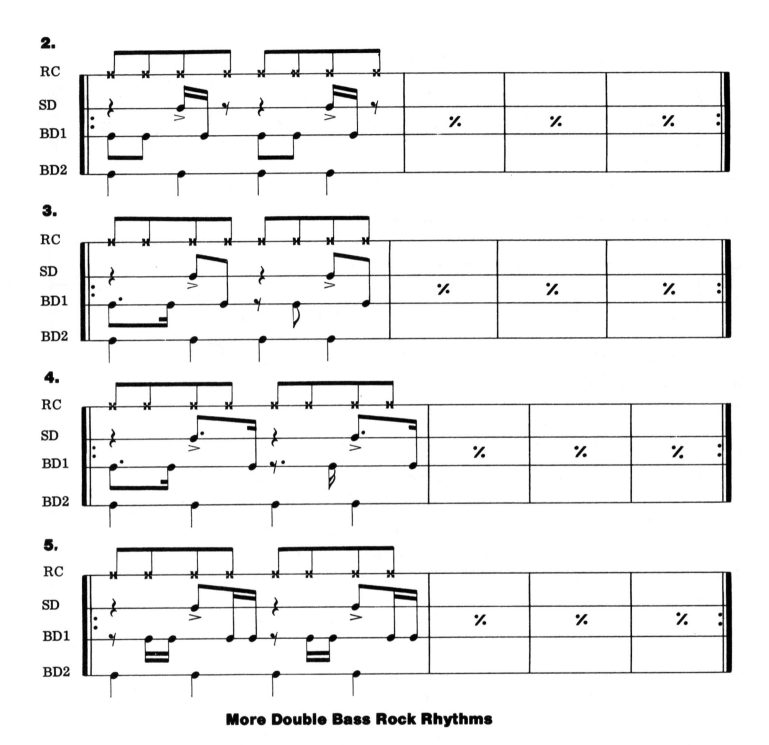

More Double Bass Rock Rhythms

(Using Quarter Notes on BD2)

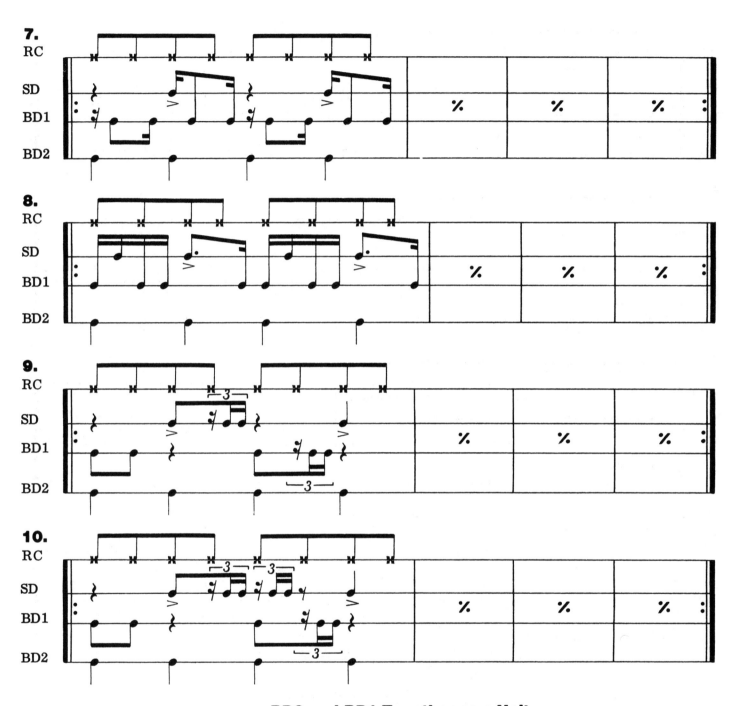

BD2 and BD1 Together as a Unit

Snare Drum on Each Beat

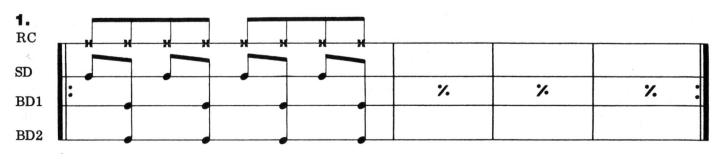

*For extra heavy rhythms of the feet.

2.

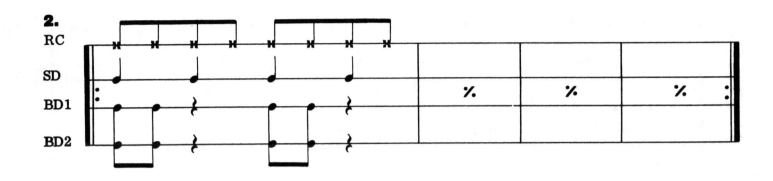

3.

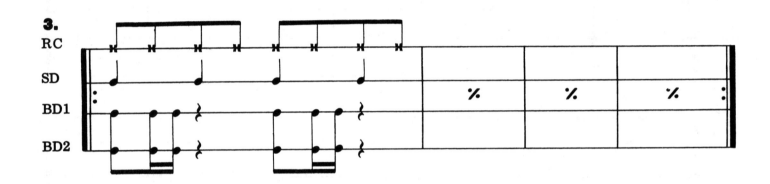

4.

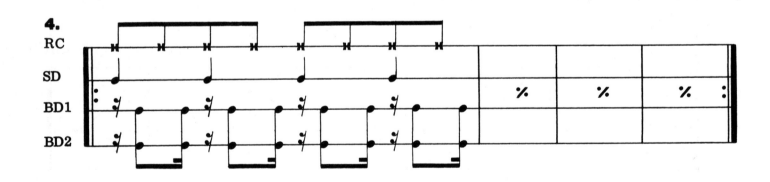

5.

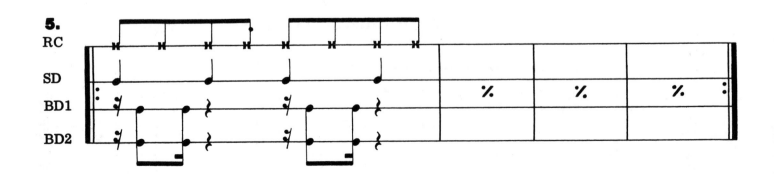

BD2 and BD1 — Together

Snare Drum on 2 and 4

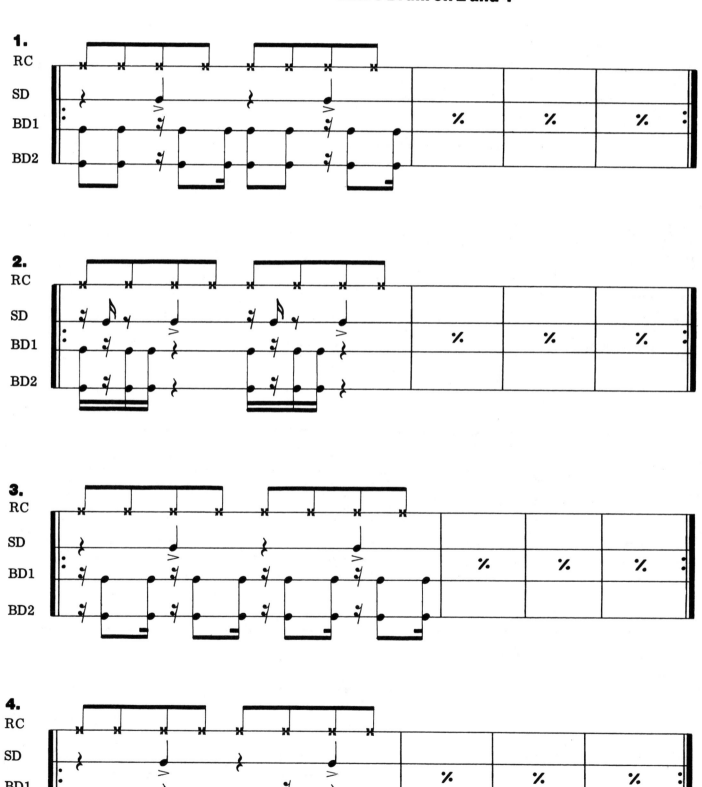

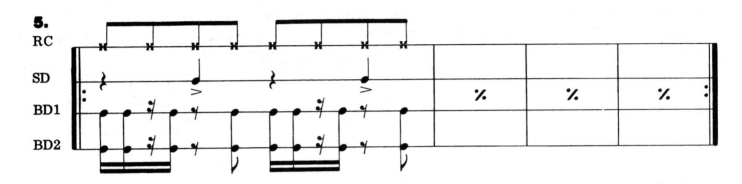

5.

Sixteen Bar Exercise

CD 1

TRK 12

Part 13

Realistic Linear Rudiments

The definition of linear is...Nothing hits together. Until now we've played patterns where different limbs play at the same time as other limbs. The following exercises will give you a new outlook on playing and will open up many new concepts for you to play.

Linear Rudiments

These rudiments should be practiced slowly at first, and gradually speed them up. These are LINEAR GROUPINGS as well as rudiments. A grouping is a group of notes that when played create a phrase or melody.

R = RIGHT HAND   L = LEFT HAND   Ⓕ = FOOT

A- The Three note grouping = R L Ⓕ   B- Four note grouping R L L Ⓕ
                          1 2 3   1 2 3 4

Use a metronome playing quarter notes to practice to!!!!

C- The Five = R L R R Ⓕ Play hand to hand over and over.
              L R L L Ⓕ
              1 2 3 4 5

D- The Six = R L R L L Ⓕ repeat over and over
              1 2 3 4 5 6

Now, practice these very seriously because these patterns are the basis for linear playing.

Putting It Together

Let's put some of these rudiments together so we can use them as grooves and fills. The first combination we will use is using the 7 and 9 grouping.

The six and three together = the nine grouping. 9= R L R L L Ⓕ R L Ⓕ
repeat, etc.   1 2 3 4 5 6 7 8 9

The four and three together = the seven grouping. 7= R L L Ⓕ R L Ⓕ repeat etc.

All linear rudiments can be played as follows to create independence. Practice all of the following ways:

1-Rights Bass Drum (right foot when you see the " Ⓕ ").

2-Left Bass Drum (left foot when you see the " Ⓕ ").

3-Alternate Bass Drums (if your first hit is a right the next Bass Drum (BD) hit is a left etc.) You can also use your left foot on your Hi-Hat.

How To Use These Rudiments

Now, in 4/4 time there are 16 sixteenth notes to a bar. So let's count our LINEAR GROUPINGS as 16th notes. We need two groupings that would sub-divide into 16. A good one to start with is the 7 and 9, together they equal 16, which equals one bar. The syncopation created by this combination is what makes this stuff interesting, fresh and new. Below are some examples of this concept: play them slow at first, then build up speed.

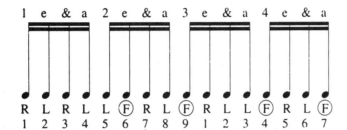

9+7=16 notes Repeat etc.

Two bar phrases sound great doing these patterns. Here are some two bar combinations. Thirty-two sixteenth notes.

2- Repeat #1 for two bars = 9-7 9-7 and play over and over. Put two bars of straight time in between the LINEAR GROUPING patterns.

2a- You can do 9-7 or reverse it to 7-9; it still has the same total of notes. (1 bar =16, 2 bars =32).

Here is the 9-7 (A), and 7-9 (B) sequences. Play A & B together as a two bar phrase

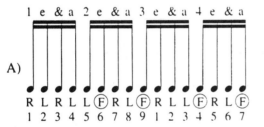
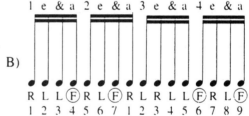

1-Once you get these down, put your right hand on the Hi-Hat, the left hand on the snare drum and play the exercise.

2-Put your left hand on the Hi-Hat and your right hand on the snare and Toms. This will create a different variation of syncopation.

Here are some more LINEAR GROUPING combinations to try: (2 bars).

#5) 9-9/7-7   #6) 7-7/9-9   #7) 7-7-2/9-7   #8) 5-5-1 (one bar)

#9) 4 bars 64 -16th notes: 4 bars 7-7-7-7 7-7-7-7-7-1 = 4 Bars
$$9 \times 7 + 1 = 64 \text{ sixteenth notes}$$

If you want to learn more about LINEAR patterns check out a video called RICK'S LICKS by Rick Gratton. This video was released by POWER ROCK DRUM SYSTEM music instructional videos.

You can order by telephone by calling 818-377-9782 for $29.95 + $3.00 handling charge, or order online at: www.powerrock.com.

NOTE: Use a metronome playing quarter notes to practice.

Now go to CD#1 and pick a song to play along with. There are no drums, so choose some of your favorite beats and play along to **Everybody's Comin'** and **Gray Day**, which are in 4/4!

This page has been left open for you to write your own rhythms. Good luck, and have fun!

RC
SD
BD

RC
SD
BD

RC
SD
BD

RC
SD
BD

RC
SD
BD

RC
SD
BD

Part 14_____

Realistic Rock 7/8 Timing

Welcome to the odd time signatures of Realistic Rock. In this section we will learn how to play in 7/8 and 9/8 time signatures. These two odd time signatures are very close when learning to play them. What makes them different are two eighth notes.

Our first odd time signature will be 7/8.

In 4/4 we have eight eighth notes in one bar and in 7/8 we have seven eighth notes in one bar.

Counting out loud and repeating each count will only increase your ability to feel natural with these odd time signatures. Once comfortable, each downbeat will be easily anticipated as if you were playing in 4/4. Emphasizing the one of each count with your bass drum will speed up the process!

The count is simple: **1, 2, 3, 4, 5, 6, sev,**... saying **SEV** instead of seven makes it easier to count so that all the counts are one syllable.

Remember—count over and over... **1, 2, 3, 4, 5, 6, sev, 1, 2, 3, 4, 5, 6, sev,** etc.

It is important to note that the 7/8 grooves will change the note values in relation to 4/4.

Example:

Eighth notes = one beat
Sixteenth notes = half a beat
Eighth notes are now counted **1, 2, 3, 4, 5, 6, sev.**
Sixteenth notes are now counted **1 &, 2 &, 3 &, 4 &, 5 &, 6 &, 7 &,** etc.
Sixteenth note triplets are now counted **1 & a, 2 & a, 3 & a, 4 & a, 5 & a, 6 & a, 7 & a,** etc.

In order to make each exercise easier to read, think of them as bars of 4/4 stopping on the count of four and where the & of four should be we now think of it as beat one... in other words, we cut off the last eighth note of the 4/4 bar.

Count **1 &, 2 &, 3 &, 4, 1 &, 2 &, 3 &, 4**—no space between **4** and **1**... when counting, as previously mentioned, emphasize the count of one (downbeat) with your bass drum in order to feel comfortable with the 7/8 time signature.

Good luck... now go to **Ex.1** and have some fun!

Realistic 7/8 Time—Eighth Notes

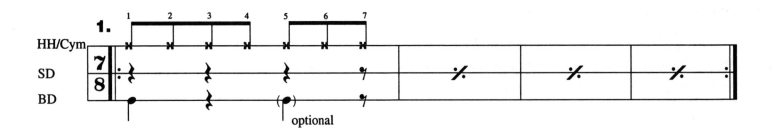

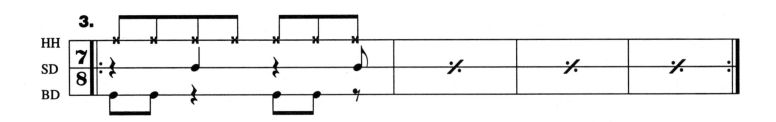

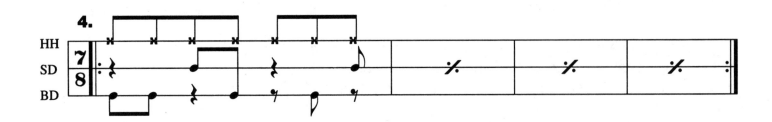

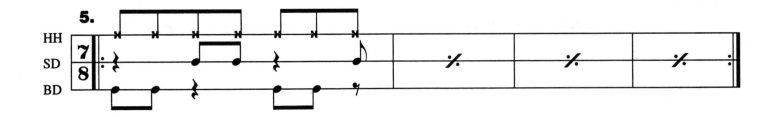

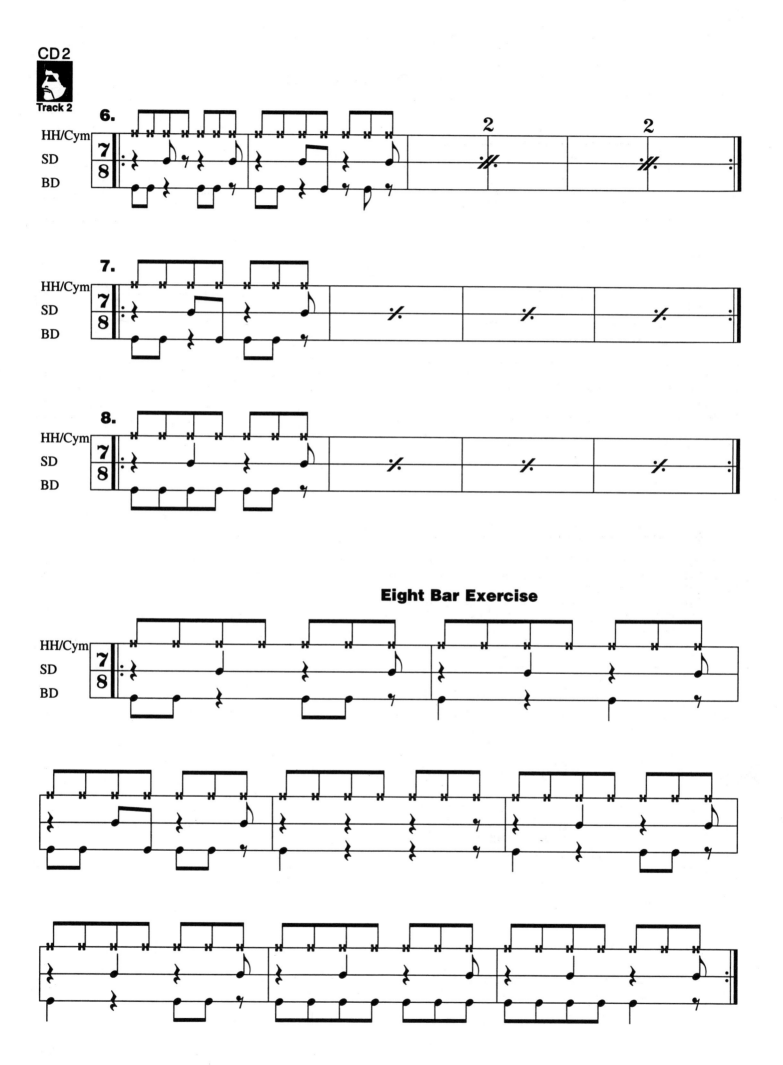

Eight Bar Exercise

Realistic 7/8 Time—Sixteenth Notes

7/8 Time—Sixteenth Notes

Eight Bar Exercise

7/8 Bonus Groove
7/8 Against 4 on the Snare

CD 2
Track 5

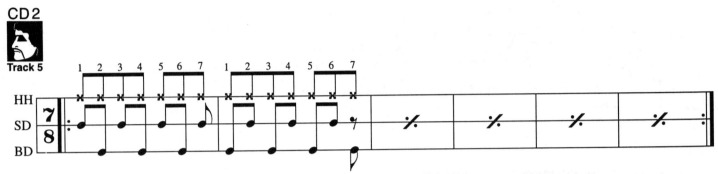

The above exercise creates a 4/4 feel on the snare even though we are playing in 7/8. This technique can and should be applied to all odd time signatures... 7/8 - 9/8 - 11/8 - 13/8, etc.

CD 2
Track 6

🞅 = Crash   Time   **7/8 Fills**   ***7/8 Fills**
                                                            Fill 1

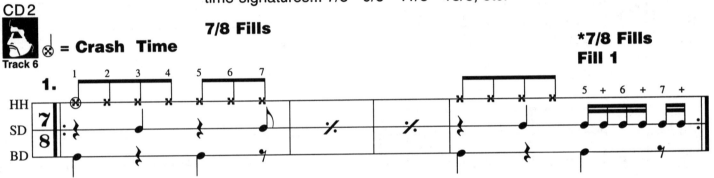

2. Fill   **Time/Groove**

3. Fill   **Time/Groove**

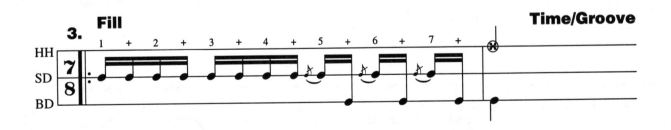

* Play fill and then play time.

7/8 Drum Fills

4.

Time/Groove

5.

Time/Groove

CD 2
Track 7

7/8 to 4/4—Four Bar Phrases

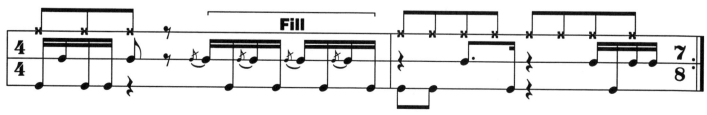

7/8 Bonus Groove

Note: On **CD 1** there is a **Play-along song** called **STASH.**
The solo is played as three bars of **7/8** and one bar of **4/4.**
Here is an example of the three bars of **7/8** and one bar of **4/4** on the **CD 1** play-along **STASH.**

CD 1

Track 15

_____**Part 15**

CD 2

Track 9

Realistic Rock 9/8 Timing

Now that you have finished the 7/8 exercises it is time to add the two eighth notes we talked about and have some fun with 9/8!

In 9/8, just like 7/8, the eighth notes are counted as one beat. There are nine eighth notes to a bar. The count is **1, 2, 3, 4, 5, 6, sev(7), 8, 9.**

Once again, keep counting out loud so that the time becomes automatic and you can feel each downbeat naturally!

Count this over and over... **1, 2, 3, 4, 5, 6, sev(7), 8, 9, 1, 2, 3, 4, 5, 6, sev(7), 8, 9,** etc.

With each count, remember to play your bass drum on the count of one (downbeat) in order to feel comfortable with 9/8, just like the way we practiced in the 7/8 section.

Once again, the eighth note gets a full beat and the sixteenth note gets half a beat. You should have the idea by now, if not, go back to the 7/8 text and review.

9/8 is the same as playing one bar of 4/4 except you now add one eighth note and count **1 &, 2 &, 3 &, 4 &, 5**—the count stops on the fifth beat... there is no **&** of **5**—the count starts over again after **5** and then immediately back to **1.**

Go for it... **Good Luck!**

Realistic 9/8 Time—Eighth Notes

7.

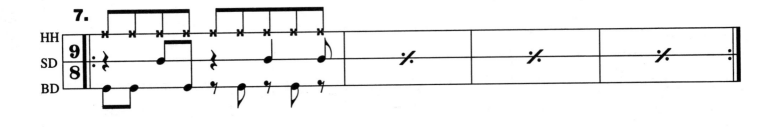

8.

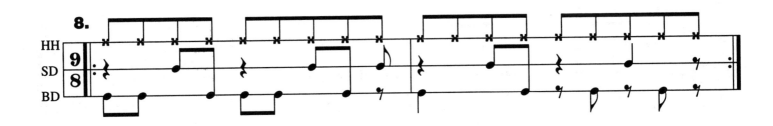

CD 2

Track 10

Eight Bar Exercise

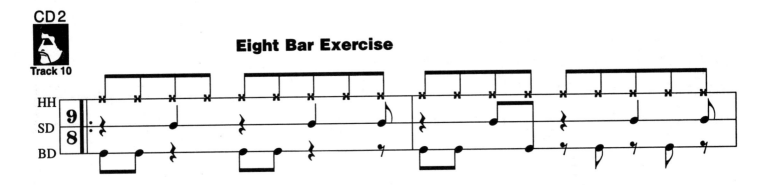

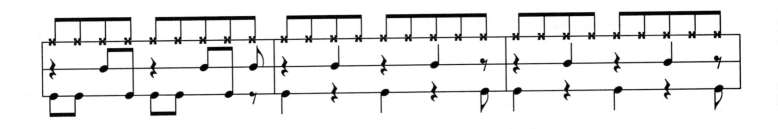

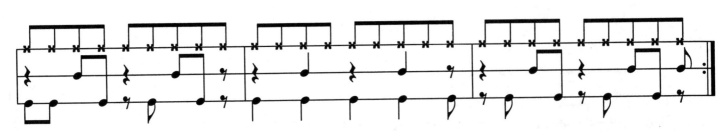

Note: Bars seven and eight imply a 4/4 time signature in the bass drum while playing in 9/8.

Realistic 9/8 Time—Sixteenth Notes

Eight Bar Exercise

9/8 Against 4 on the Snare
9/8 Bonus

CD 2

Track 13

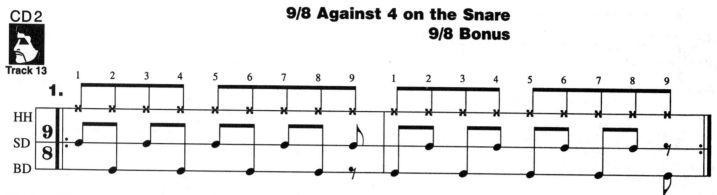

Note: The snare plays on all of the downbeats in the first bar and then automatically switches to the off-beats in the second bar.

CD 2

Track 14

9/8 Drum Fills

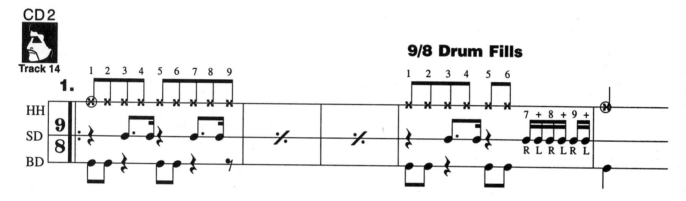

*Fills

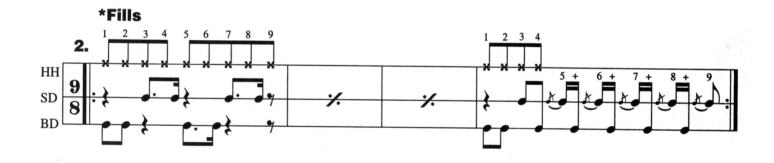

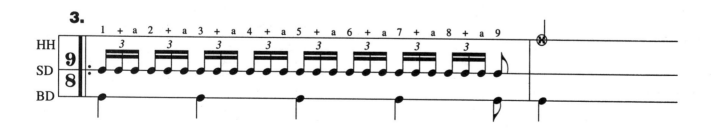

* Play Groove and apply fills then back to Groove.

Realistic Rock 9/8
9/8 to 4/4 Time

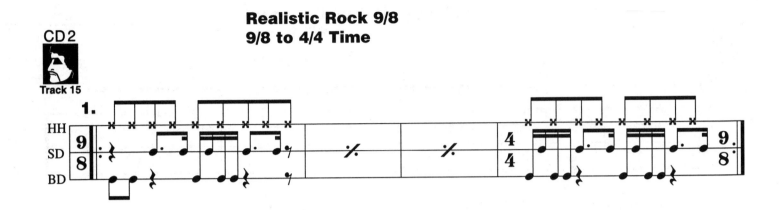

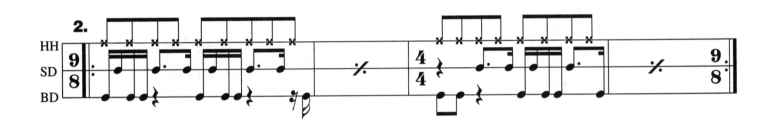

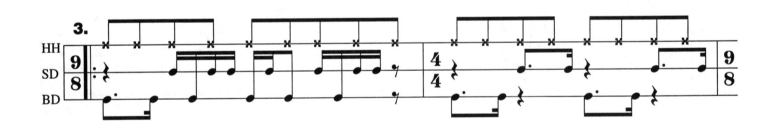

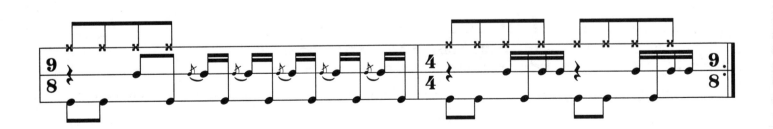

CD 2

Track 17

Part 16

Combinations

Cymbals/Snare Drum

In this section we will explore various hand and foot combinations that can be played in a variety of musical situations.

Here we will present these "cutting edge" combinations as drum fills using triplets and sixteenth notes. Once you are comfortable with them, you will quickly discover how melodic and powerful your drumming will become which is a trademark of all great rock drummers!

Combination #1

Each exercise will include the count with the appropriate sticking and foot combination written underneath. Play them as sixteenth notes with an **even** and **steady** flow!

Ex. 1

LISTEN TO THE **FILL** ON THE **CD.**

	1	e	&	a	2	e	&	a	3	e	repeat over and over
	1	2	1	2	1	2	1	2	3	4	
Hands	R	L			R	L					
Feet			R	L			R	L	R	L	

Practice slowly at first then build up speed.

Ex. 2   **Played as sixteenth notes**

CHECK OUT THE **SLOW** and **FAST** VERSIONS ON THE **CD.**

	1	e	&	a	2	e	&	a	3	e	&	a	4	e	&	a	repeat
	1	2	1	2	1	2	1	2	3	4	1	2	1	2	3	4	
Hands	R	L			R	L					R	L					
Feet			R	L			R	L	R	L			R	L	R	L	

Practice slowly at first to build up speed.

Ex. 3

CHECK OUT THE **SLOW** and **FAST** VERSIONS ON THE **CD.**

	1	e	&	a	2	e	&	a	3	e	&	a	4	e	&	a
	1	2	3	4	1	2	3	4	1	2	3	4	1	2	3	4
Hands	R	L	R	L					R	L	R	L				
Feet					R	L	R	L					R	L	R	L

Combinations #2

The combinations below are played with the hands on the snare or toms and two China cymbals. The China cymbals are to be played together with your bass drums. As you gradually increase your speed, the short "staccato" sound of the Chinas will help your momentum until you are playing these patterns as fast and as clean as you want.

In order to feel comfortable with these patterns, it is recommended that you first learn to play the patterns between the snare and the double bass drums and gradually introduce the China cymbals and then the toms.

These combinations are similar to Ex.1 except the bass drums are now answering the hand patterns.

Practice Between Snare and Bass Drums... Play all sixteenth notes as even strokes.

Ex. 1

1	e	&	a	2	e	&	a	repeat
1	2	1	2	1	2	3	4	
Hands R	L	R	L	R	L	R	L	
Feet		R	L			R	L	

CC = China Cymbal

LISTEN TO THE **FILL** ON THE **CD.**

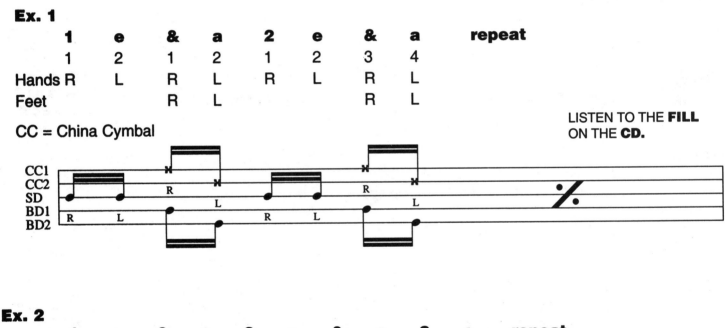

Ex. 2

1	e	&	a	2	e	&	a	3	e	repeat
1	2	3	4	1	2	1	2	3	4	
Hands R	L	R	L	R	L	R	L	R	L	
Feet		R	L			R	L	R	L	

Play these slow at first then build up speed. After you build up speed... Practice playing the hands and feet together with the China cymbals. (See Below)

LISTEN TO THE **FILL** ON THE **CD.**

Ex. 3

	1	e	&	a	2	e	&	a	repeat
	1	2	1	2	1	2	3	4	
Hands	R	L	R	L	R	L	R	L	
Feet					R	L	R	L	

LISTEN TO THE **FILL**
ON THE **CD.**

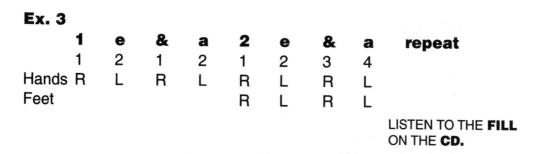

CD 2

Track 19

Combinations with Triplets

Play evenly as triplets.

Practice slowly at first and build up speed!

Ex. 1

	1	&	a	2	&	a	3	&	a	4	&	a
	1	2	3	1	2	3	1	2	3	1	2	3
Hands	R	L	R				R	L	R			
Feet				R	L	R				R	L	R

Ex. 2

	1	&	a	2	&	a	3	&	a	4	&	a
	1	2	3	1	2	3	1	2	3	1	2	3
Hands	R	L			R	L			R	L		
Feet			R	L			R	L			R	L

Ex. 3

	1	&	a	2	&	a	3	&	a	4	&	a
	1	2	3	1	2	3	1	2	3	1	2	3
Hands	L	R	L				L	R	L			
Feet				R	L	R				R	L	R

Note: Play **Ex. 2** with the **R L** on the feet together with the China
cymbals.

Ex. 4

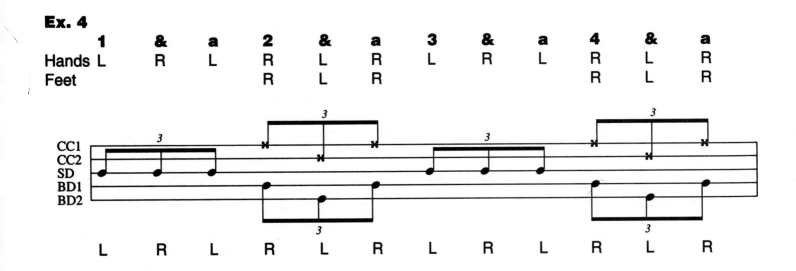

LISTEN TO THE **FILL** ON THE **CD.**

The China cymbals are to be played together with the bass drums.

CD 2

Track 20

Part 17

Rave / Dance

Here are some of the basic **Rave** patterns played today. The opening and closing Hi-Hat and the steady quarter notes on the bass drum are the "trademark" of these rhythms. Practice at **160** Tempos or more!

+ = closed Hi-Hat
0 = open Hi-Hat

Note: Practice all of the exercises opening the Hi-Hat on all the **upbeats** or **&'s** with these two examples.

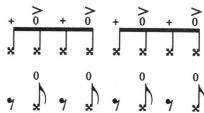

DISCOGRAPHY

Artist	Album	Record Label
Vanilla Fudge	Vanilla Fudge	Atco/Atlantic
Vanilla Fudge	The Beat Goes On	Atco/Atlantic
Vanilla Fudge	Renaissance	Atco/Atlantic
Vanilla Fudge	Near the Beginning	Atco/Atlantic
Vanilla Fudge	Rock and Roll	Atco/Atlantic
Vanilla Fudge	2001	Hyperspace
Vanilla Fudge	Mystery	Atco
Vanilla Fudge	Live, Best of	Rhino
Vanilla Fudge	Out Through the In Door	
Cactus	Cactus	Atco/Atlantic
Cactus	One Way or Another	Atco/Atlantic
Cactus	Restrictions	Atco/Atlantic
Cactus	'Ot 'N Sweaty	Atco/Atlantic
Cactus	Collection/Cactology	Rhino
Cactus	Cactus Music/Cacuts V plus DVD	Fuel
Jeff Beck, Tim Bogert, Carmine Appice	Beck, Bogert & Appice	Epic/CBS
Jeff Beck	Beckology	Epic
KGB	KGB	MCA
KGB	Motion	MCA
Rod Stewart & Group	Foot Loose & Fancy Free	Warner Bros.
Rod Stewart & Group	Blondes Have More Fun	Warner Bros.
Rod Stewart & Group	Foolish Behavior	Warner Bros.
Rod Stewart & Group	Tonight I'm Yours	Warner Bros.
Rod Stewart	Rod Stewart Anthology	Geffen
Stanley Clarke	Modern Man	CBS
Paul Stanley	Kiss – Paul Stanley	Casablanca/Polygram
Ron Wood	1, 2, 3, 4	CBS
Carmine Appice	Carmine Appice/Rockers	Pasha/CBS
Carmine Appice	Channel Mind Radio	Polydor KK
Carmine Appice	Guitar Zeus I	Apollion, No Bull (Europe)
Carmine Appice	Guitar Zeus II	
Carmine Appice	Guitar Zeus (Japan)	Rock Records (Japan)
Carmine Appice	Guitar Zeus Conquering Heroes	Fuel
Ted Nugent	Nugent	Atlantic
King Kobra	Ready to Strike	Capitol
King Kobra	Thrill of a Lifetime	Capitol
King Kobra	King Kobra III	Rocker
King Kobra	Lost Years	Cleopatra Records
King Kobra	Hollywood Trash	MTM (Europe)
King Kobra	TBA	Fuel
Soundtrack/TriStar	Iron Eagle	Capitol
Pink Floyd	Momentary Lapse of Reason	CBS
Blue Murder	Blue Murder	Geffen
Blue Murder	Nothin' but Trouble	Geffen
Brad Gillis	Gillrock Ranch	Guitar Recordings
Jeff Watson	Lone Ranger	Shrapnel
Mothers Army	Mothers Army (Japan)	Appollion (Fems)
Pearl	East Meets West	Polydor KK
Pearl	4 Infinity	East West
Pearl	Live in Japan	Distribute/Sony
Char, Bogert & Appice	CBA Live in Japan	Polydor KK
Derringer & Appice	Party Tested	Boardwalk Records
Derringer, Bogert & Appice	DBA Doin' Business As	SPV (Europe)
Travers & Appice	It Takes a Lot of Balls	
Travers & Appice	Live – Keep on Rockin'	Fuel

ENDORSEMENTS

DDRUM DRUMS
VIC FIRTH SIGNATURE STICKS
AQUARIAN SIGNATURE HEADS
SHURE MICS
RHYTHM TECH
ZOOM PRODUCTS
LP PERCUSSION

DW PEDALS
ROLAND ELECTRONICS
SABIAN CYMBALS
CALZONE CASES
PROTECHTOR CASES
DEAN GUITARS

PERFORMANCE SET-UP

ddrum Drums
- Two 24" x 14" bass drums; 12" x 8" and 13" x 9" rack toms; 16" x 16" and 16" x 18" floor toms
- 14" x 5" Carmine Appice Signature brass snare drum
- 15" Carmine Appice "Lampshade" cymbal

Sabian Cymbals
- 17" and 19" Carmine Appice Signature Chinas
- 21" Carmine Appice Signature ride
- 18" and 20" HH crashes
- 14" HH hi-hats

DW Pedals
- 5000 Series single and double pedals
- Hardware

For more instructional material produced by Carmine Appice, go to:
www.powerrock.com
Featuring DVDs by:
Tris Imbodin (Chicago)
Slim Jim Phantom (Stray Cats)
Carmine and Vinny Appice: *Drum Wars* and more…

CARMINE & DDRUM

THE WORLD'S GREATEST ROCK DRUMMER PLAYS THE WORLD'S GREATEST DRUMS

CARMINE APPICE SIGNATURE BRASS SNARE

CARMINE APPICE "LAMPSHADE" CYMBAL

CARMINE APPICE SIGNATURE 80'S KIT

ddrum.
JOIN THE REVOLUTION AT
WWW.DDRUM.COM

ddrum.
ACOUSTIC & ELECTRONIC DRUM PRODUCTS SINCE 1981

FOR EVERYTHING
CARMINE VISIT
WWW.CARMINEAPPICE.COM

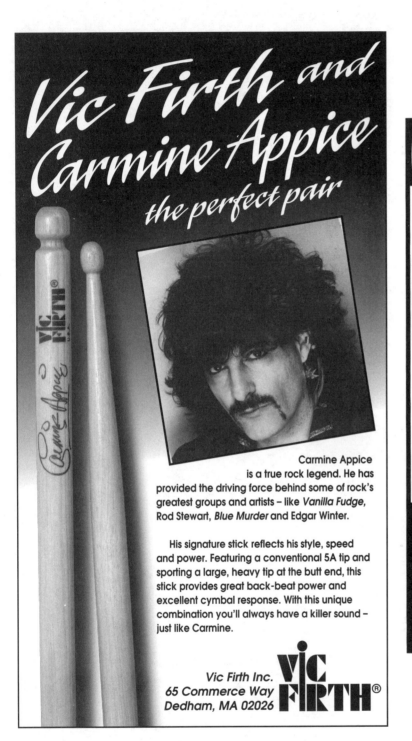
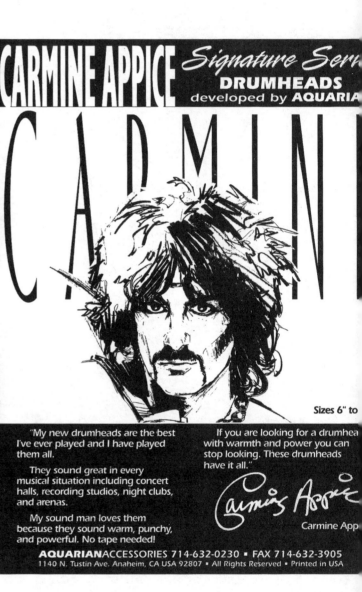

www.sabian.com

Carmine Appice

"Carmine Appice set the foundation for heavy drumming... before Bonham, before Ian Paice...before anyone else."
—Rick Van Horn, *Modern Drummer*

Ultimate Realistic Rock, Complete DVD

(25717) 2 DVDs

Hosted by Leslie Gold, the Radiochick, this jam-packed 2-DVD set includes step-by-step instruction through each section of Carmine Appice's award-winning book, *Ultimate Realistic Rock*. Features instruction by Carmine himself with special guests Kenny Aronoff, John Tempesta, Vinny Appice, Bobby Rondinelli, and Rick Gratton.

Also included are performances with guitar legend Pat Travers, a "you supply the drums" play-along section, and a Carmine Appice rockumentary chronicling Carmine's celebrated career in the music business.

Ultimate Realistic Rock Mega Pak

(27750) Book, 2 CDs, and DVD

Carmine's award-winning book is now available with the DVD *Ultimate Realistic Rock, The Basics*, featuring instruction through selected exercises by Carmine Appice and special guests Kenny Aronoff, John Tempesta, Vinny Appice, Bobby Rondinelli, and Rick Gratton.

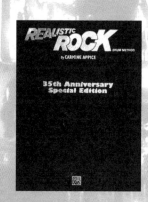

Realistic Rock 35th Anniversary Special Edition

(27666) Book and Enhanced CD

This 35th anniversary special edition of *Realistic Rock* brings you the material from its first edition printing in 1972, complete with original cover art and photos. Also included is an enhanced CD with a Carmine Appice video rockumentary and performance footage with the band Cactus.

ALSO AVAILABLE

Ultimate Play-Along Drum Trax: Carmine Appice Guitar Zeus

(0739B) Book and 2 CDs

This play-along package includes Carmine's drum parts selected from the CDs *Guitar Zeus I* and *II*, which highlight the monster guitar talents of Ted Nugent, Paul Gilbert, Stevie Salas, Yngwie Malmsteen, Richie Sambora, Neal Schon, and Zakk Wylde.

Realistic Rock for Kids
My 1st Rock & Roll Drum Method

(0663B) Book and 2 CDs

Here's the kid's version of the award-winning drum method *Realistic Rock*. Perfect for all kids, this one shows them how to play rock & roll drums the quick and easy way.

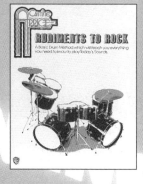

Rudiments to Rock

(DF0004) Book

This book is for beginners. It starts with the most basic fundamentals of drumming, then gradually progresses by introducing various rudiments with focus on developing and coordinating the hands, feet, and mind.

Realistic Rock for Kids
My 1st Rock & Roll Drum Method

(34266) DVD

Just like in his classic award-winning drum method *Ultimate Realistic Rock*, Carmine has made learning to play the drums FUN and EASY! Hosted by Carmine and his star pupil, 12-year-old contest winner Pete Biggiani, this DVD will teach you all you need to know to get started on the drums.

Visit alfred.com/drums for more info.